The Governance of Regulators

# Driving Performance at Portugal's Energy Services Regulatory Authority

**Please cite this publication as:**
OECD (2021), *Driving Performance at Portugal's Energy Services Regulatory Authority*, The Governance of Regulators, OECD Publishing, Paris, *https://doi.org/10.1787/05fb2fae-en*.

ISBN 978-92-64-91152-9 (print)
ISBN 978-92-64-70820-4 (pdf)

The Governance of Regulators
ISSN 2415-1432 (print)
ISSN 2415-1440 (online)

**Photo credits:** Cover © Leigh Prather - Fotolia.com, © Mr.Vander - Fotolia.com, © magann - Fotolia.com.

Corrigenda to publications may be found on line at: *www.oecd.org/about/publishing/corrigenda.htm*.

# Foreword

Regulatory agencies are key actors in the delivery of good regulatory outcomes. Their role brings together several powers: rule-making, market monitoring, enforcement and sanctioning. Regulators are at the delivery end of the policy cycle and their job is a complex one, as it requires neutral engagement with actors that may well have inherently competing interests (such as government, current and future actors in the markets, and consumers). At the same time, markets are changing at a significant pace, due to new technologies, shifts in consumer needs and preferences, new policy priorities and the profound changes brought by the coronavirus pandemic. These changes are accompanied by high public expectations that independent economic regulators will be transparent and accountable in their decisions and actions.

Regulators will need robust technical competence and capacity, transparency, autonomy and constructive engagement with stakeholders to navigate this complex landscape. The good governance of regulators helps ensure that regulatory decisions are made on an objective and consistent basis, without conflict of interest, bias or undue influence. The rapid change in markets also requires regulators to balance their role of providing predictability and stability with the objective of facilitating and supporting investment and innovation.

To support regulators as they face these challenges, the OECD has developed a framework to assess and strengthen their organisational performance and governance structures. The framework analyses regulators' internal and external governance, including their organisational structures, behaviour, accountability, business processes, reporting and performance management, as well as role clarity, relationships, distribution of powers and responsibilities with other government and non-government stakeholders.

This report applies this Performance Assessment Framework (PAFER) to Portugal's Energy Services Regulatory Authority (ERSE). It finds that the ERSE is a mature and well-respected regulator, which has shown agility in taking on new roles over the past two and a half decades in support of the development of the Portuguese energy sector and outcomes for consumers. ERSE also demonstrated an advanced use of good regulatory practices through its three consultative councils, which act as a forum for creating consensus among key stakeholders.

This report is part of the OECD work programme on the governance of regulators and regulatory policy, led by the OECD Network of Economic Regulators and the OECD Regulatory Policy Committee, with the support of the Regulatory Policy Division of the OECD Directorate of Public Governance. The Directorate's mission is to help government at all levels design and implement strategic, evidence-based and innovative policies that support sustainable economic and social development. The report was presented to the OECD Network of Economic Regulators (NER) for comments and approval at its 15th meeting in November 2020.

# Acknowledgements

This report was co-ordinated and drafted by Martha Baxter and Ana Simion, under the guidance of Anna Pietikainen. Alexis Durand and Claire Léger carried out initial preparatory work. The review benefited from the direction and support of Elsa Pilichowski, Director, János Bertók, Deputy Director, OECD Public Governance Directorate (GOV), and of Nick Malyshev, Head of the Regulatory Policy Division in GOV. Comments were provided by Nick Malyshev, Daniel Trnka, Marie-Gabrielle De Liedekerke and Supriya Trivedi, OECD, Peter Journeay-Kaler and Alessio Scanziani, International Energy Agency. Bruno Damásio, Professor at NOVA Information Management School, New University of Lisbon provided guidance in the preparation of missions. Jennifer Stein co-ordinated the editorial process and Andrea Uhrhammer provided editorial support.

Three peer reviewers provided extensive input and feedback throughout the development of the review: Darryl Biggar, Special Economic Adviser, Australian Competition and Consumer Commission (ACCC), Australia; Laura Brien, Director of Water and Compliance, Commission for Regulation of Utilities (CRU), Ireland; and Emma Närvä, Deputy Director for International Affairs and Senior Policy Adviser, Swedish Post and Telecom Authority (PTS), Sweden.

The report would not have been possible without the support of ERSE and its staff. The team would in particular like to thank the following colleagues for their assistance in collecting data and information, support to organising the team's missions to Portugal, for their flexibility in conducting work remotely, as well as for providing feedback at different stages of the review: Maria Cristina Portugal, Chair of the Board of Directors, Mariana Pereira and Pedro Verdelho, Members of the Board of Directors, Natalie McCoy, Head of International Relations, and Ana Filipa Santos, Technical Officer in the Board of Directors Support Office. Interviews and comments from the various ERSE departments, government, industry and civil society stakeholders during the review process contributed to the analysis presented in the report.

# Table of contents

## Tables



## Figures



## Boxes

# Abbreviations and acronyms

**ACCC** Australian Competition and Consumer Commission

**ACE** Support to the Energy Consumers Office (ERSE internal department)

**ACER** Agency for the Co-operation of Energy Regulators

**AdC** Competition Authority (*Autoridade da Concorrência*)

**ADR** Alternative Dispute Resolution

**AEMO** Australian Energy Market Operator

**AER** Australian Energy Regulator

**ANACOM** National Authority for Communications (*Autoridade Nacional de Comunicações)*

**ANEEL** Brazilian Electricity Regulatory Agency (*Agência Nacional de Energia Elétrica*)

**ANMP** National Association of Portuguese Municipalities (*Associação Nacional de Municípios Portugueses*)

**ASAE** Economic and Food Safety Authority (*Autoridade de Segurança Alimentar e Económica*)

**ASEAN** Association of Southeast Asian Nations

**AT** Tributary Authority *(Autoridade Tributária)*

**CBA** Cost-benefit Analysis

**CEER** Council of European Energy Regulators

**CISPN** National Petroleum System Installation Commission (ERSE internal department)

**CMVM** Portuguese Securities Market Commission (*Comissão do Mercado de Valores Mobiliários*)

**CNCS** National Center for Cybersecurity *(Centro Nacional de Cibersegurança)*

**CNMC** National Commission for Markets and Competition (*Comisión Nacional de los Mercados*)

**CNMV** Spanish Securities Market Commission (*Comisión Nacional del Mercado de Valores*)

**CR MIBEL** Board of Regulators of the Iberian Electricity Market

**CRE** The French Energy Regulator (*Commission de Régulation de l'Énergie*)

**CRESAP** Public Administration Recruitment and Selection Committee *(Comissão de Recrutamento e Seleção para a Administração Pública)*

**CRU** Commission for Regulation of Utilities

**DAG** General Administration Division (ERSE internal department)

**DCE** Energy Consumers Division (ERSE internal department)

**DCP** Costs and Revenues Division (ERSE internal department)

**DEA** Data Envelopment Analysis (ERSE internal department)

**DGC** Directorate-General for Consumer Affairs (*Direção-Geral Consumidor)*

| | |
|---|---|
| **DGEG** | Directorate General for Energy and Geology (*Direção Geral de Energia e Geologia*) |
| **DGR** | The Directorate-General for Regulation (ERSE internal department) |
| **DIR** | Infrastructure and Network Division (ERSE internal department) |
| **DMC** | Markets and Competition Division (previously Markets and Consumers Division, ERSE internal departments) |
| **DSJ** | Legal Division (ERSE internal department) |
| **DSO** | Distribution System Operator |
| **DTP** | Pricing and Tariffs Division (ERSE internal department) |
| **EDP** | Electricidade de Portugal |
| **EISG** | Energy Intermarket Surveillance Group (ERSE internal department) |
| **ENMC** | National Entity for the Fuel Market, National Entity for the Fuel Market (*Entidade Nacional para o Mercado de Combustíveis*) |
| **ENSE** | National Entity for the Energy Sector (*Entidade Nacional para o Setor Energético*) |
| **ENTSO-E** | European Network of Transmission System Operators for Electricity |
| **ENTSOG** | European Network of Transmission System Operators for Gas |
| **ERSE** | Energy Services Regulatory Authority (*Entidade Reguladora dos Serviços Energéticos*) |
| **ESCOSA** | Essential Services Commission of South Australia |
| **EU** | European Union |
| **FCA** | Financial Conduct Authority |
| **FDUNL** | Faculty of Law of the New University of Lisbon *(Faculdade de Direito da Universidade Nova de Lisboa)* |
| **GACA** | Support to the Board of Directors Office (ERSE internal department) |
| **GDPR** | General Data Protection Regime |
| **GGI** | Internal Management Office (ERSE internal department) |
| **GRI** | Office of International Relations (ERSE internal department) |
| **IDEP** | Special Projects Development Office (ERSE internal department) |
| **IEA** | International Energy Agency |
| **IESO** | Independent Electricity System Operator |
| **IMT** | Institute for Mobility and Transport *(Instituto da Mobilidade e dos Transportes)* |
| **IST** | The Superior Tehcnological Institute *(Instituto Superior Técnico)* |
| **KPIs** | Key Performance Indicators |
| **LNEG** | National Laboratory of Energy and Geology (*Laboratório Nacional de Energia e Geologia*) |
| **LNG** | Liquefied Natural Gas |
| **MAAC** | Ministry of the Environment and Climate *(Ministério do Ambiente e da Ação Climática*) |
| **MIBEL** | Iberian Electricity Market |
| **NCEP** | National Energy Climate Plan |
| **NZCC** | New Zealand Commerce Commission |
| **OECD** | Organisation for Economic Co-operation and Development |
| **Ofgem** | UK's Office of Gas and Electricity Markets |
| **OMIE** | Operador del Mercado Ibérico de Energía |

| | |
|---|---|
| **OMIP** | Operador do Mercado Ibérico de Energía Polo Portugues |
| **OROC** | Portuguese Institute of Statutory Auditors (*Ordem dos revisores oficiais de conta*) |
| **PAFER** | Performance Assessment Framework for Economic Regulators |
| **PTS** | Swedish Post and Telecom Authority |
| **PV** | Solar Photovoltaics |
| **RELOP** | Association of Portuguese Speaking Energy Regulatory Entities |
| **REMIT** | EU Regulation on Wholesale Energy Market Integrity and Transparency |
| **REN** | Rede Elétrica Nacional |
| **SIMER** | ERSE Information System for Market Analysis *(Sistema de Informação de Mercados)* |
| **SME** | Small and medium-sized enterprises |
| **TPES** | Total Primary Energy Supply |
| **TSO** | Transmission System Operator |
| **UTAIL** | Technical Unit for Legislative Impact Assessment |

# Executive summary

The Energy Services Regulatory Authority (*Entidade Reguladora dos Serviços Energéticos*, ERSE) is Portugal's independent economic regulator for the energy sector. The regulator was established in 1997, concurrently with the liberalisation of the Portuguese electricity market. Throughout its existence, ERSE has provided stability and predictability to the sector. By virtue of technical expertise and capacity, it is currently highly regarded by stakeholders.

The energy sector in Portugal has been transformed over the past 25 years. During this time, ERSE has demonstrated flexibility and has been successful in taking on new roles, matched by a proven agility to adapt governance and regulatory practices to new trends and challenges, most recently during the COVID-19 pandemic. Such experience will continue to be important for the regulation of a rapidly changing sector, driven both by technological progress and the decarbonisation of the Portuguese economy. ERSE's advanced stakeholder engagement practice, in the form of its consultative councils, will also continue to play a crucial role in delivering on its mandate.

Within such a context, ERSE will need to continue to be forward looking in its decisions and facilitate experimentation and innovation, while maintaining the strong sense of historic continuity and predictability. Such a vision, and its connection to the wider national context, will need to be accompanied by better monitoring against the regulator's strategic objectives, as well as communication of its performance to a wide range of stakeholders to further demonstrate the value of ERSE and the merits of independent economic regulation.

## Role and objectives of ERSE

ERSE has handled the recurrent expansion of its mandate effectively: from regulating only the electricity market upon its creation, to the addition of regulatory roles for gas, electric mobility and, most recently, fuels. ERSE's activities range beyond national borders, with an active role in the Iberian Electricity Market (MIBEL), in collaboration with the Portuguese financial markets regulator and their Spanish counterparts.

A four-year strategic plan sets out the objectives for ERSE's regulatory activities. The strategic plan reflects the highly technical work of the regulator, but misses the opportunity to project ERSE's vision and use the strategic framework to bring the message of its value to a wider audience.

### *Key recommendations*

- Reinforce the strategic framework of ERSE by introducing a greater focus on outcomes and more accessible language at all levels. This can be undertaken for the regulator's next strategic plan.
- Strengthen ERSE's identity as a forward-looking regulatory authority, encouraging its appetite for experimentation and flexibility, including identifying areas where more risks can be taken and innovations tested.

## Input

ERSE is funded mainly through contributions from the industry. The fees are defined by ERSE according to criteria set out in legislation, contributing to the regulator's independence. After the 2009 financial crisis, a number of government austerity measures affected ERSE, such as the retention in the state budget of any ERSE budget surplus, the need for government authorisation to introduce new budget lines, and salary cuts and freezes. There is some concern that the anticipated economic effect of the COVID-19 crisis might prompt the introduction of similar measures.

The ERSE workforce is experienced, knowledgeable and technically proficient. Currently, ERSE needs government authorisation for any increase in headcount, leading to a lengthy recruitment process that may hinder its agility in bringing in new skill sets.

### *Key recommendations*

- Take steps to build a constructive, 'no surprises' relationship with the executive and legislative, by initiating structured dialogue with the executive in order to set expectations on work priorities.
- Advocate for lifting of certain practices that limit the financial autonomy of the regulator and anticipate future challenges.

## Process

The three-member Board has vast responsibilities, combining both strategic and executive functions, which might reduce the Board's capacity to focus on strategic matters. Board members are limited to one term, with terms staggered at 6 months; this means that it is possible for ERSE to have an entirely new board within 18 months. This may undermine continuity in its leadership and strategic direction.

The regulator's teams are structured by function rather than sector, which enables ERSE to respond with agility to rapid sector changes. The current process of internal restructuring combined with the recent expansion of the workforce highlights the need to consolidate the internal culture of the regulator.

The engagement mechanisms at ERSE are varied. Significantly, ERSE makes use of three consultative councils that allow stakeholders within the energy sector to share information and viewpoints and reach consensus. The councils also ensure that ERSE's decision making is more transparent and robust.

### *Key recommendations*

- Advocate increasing the minimum time required between board appointments from six months to at least one year.
- Invest in the Board's strategic, outward-looking role, dedicating more time to monitoring future challenges and opportunities in the industry.
- Embed institutional renewal in the internal restructuring process and take the opportunity to strengthen the regulator's focus on innovation and foresight.
- Continue with the highly positive practice of consultative councils and preserve their value through proportionate use.

## Output and outcome

ERSE regularly collects data from market actors. Whilst procedures ensure that companies do not receive multiple data requests from different divisions of the regulator, there is no central portal that enables regulated companies to submit their information. A new cross-regulators platform is used for the supervision of petroleum and biofuels sectors, but has not yet been extended to electricity and natural gas.

The regulator does not report on its own performance against a set of comprehensive indicators, but work is underway to define associated performance indicators for the current strategic plan.

### *Key recommendations*

- Reduce regulatory burdens for the sector by streamlining data collection and collaborating on a "one-stop shop" across the energy sector.
- Monitor ERSE's own performance using the strategic framework to define performance indicators for the organisation.
- Use reporting as an opportunity to showcase the value of independent economic regulation to key external stakeholders.

# Assessment and recommendations

## Introduction

This performance assessment review looks at the external and internal governance arrangements of Portugal's Energy Services Regulatory Authority (*Entidade Reguladora dos Serviços Energéticos*, ERSE) and presents policy recommendations that aim to improve the performance of the regulator. The document builds on the work of a virtual peer policy mission that took place from 15 to 19 June 2020.[1] It was presented for discussion by the OECD Network of Economic Regulators (NER) at its meeting on 17 November 2020.

ERSE is Portugal's independent economic regulator for the electricity, natural gas and fuel sectors and the electric mobility network. It started operations in 1997 as the Regulatory Entity of the Electric Sector in tandem with the liberalisation of the Portuguese electricity sector. The regulator has provided stability and predictability to the sector over the years, and, thanks to its technical expertise and capacity, is highly regarded by stakeholders in the sector and is widely seen as a strong asset to the regulatory system. Over the years, the regulator has demonstrated flexibility and has been successful in taking on new roles. This has been matched by a proven agility to adapt governance and regulatory practice to new trends and challenges, most recently the COVID-19 pandemic. Agility will continue to be important in the post-COVID economy and more generally for the regulation of a rapidly changing sector, driven both by technological progress and policy for the decarbonisation of the Portuguese economy. In this context, ERSE will need to continue to be forward-looking in its decisions and strive to facilitate experimentation and innovation, while maintaining the strong sense of historic continuity, stability and predictability. Strengthened co-ordination and clarity of roles, as well stability of the regulator's resourcing framework, will be necessary building blocks of this approach and will require increased dialogue with the executive. Finally, monitoring progress towards the regulator's strategic objectives and communicating the results of its performance to a wide range of stakeholders will further demonstrate the value of ERSE and the merits of independent economic regulation.

## Role and objectives

### *Mandate*

**As Portugal's economic regulator for electricity, natural gas, fuels and electric mobility, ERSE provides stability and confidence in the sector through transparent and predictable decisions.** ERSE's activity is most developed in the fields of electricity and natural gas regulation, in line with European legislation that has been adopted for these sectors over the last 25 years. ERSE's objectives, clearly set out in legislation, are to: i) protect consumers; ii) ensure compliance of regulated entities with public service and other obligations; iii) ensure market integrity; iv) promote service quality; v) ensure competition between market players; vi) and resolve disputes between regulated entities and between consumers and market actors.

**ERSE has approached the expansion of its mandate to the fuels sector effectively, overcoming several challenges.** The law has expanded the sectors overseen by ERSE three times since its establishment: to natural gas in 2002, the electric mobility network in 2012 and the fuels sector in 2018.

The new responsibilities in the fuels sector mark a departure from ERSE's traditional work of regulating natural monopolies in network industries. In the fuels sector, ERSE is responsible for regulating downstream markets. Regulation in the oil products and biofuels sectors relies largely on *ex post* regulation, with the Competition Authority playing a major role until 2018. However, in the context of the energy transition, there are benefits to bringing fuels and biofuels within ERSE's remit and it enables the regulator to have a holistic view of the different segments of the energy sector. The new role brought with it challenges of role clarity and co-ordination with other public bodies that were already active in the fuels sector, but ERSE has found workable solutions to overcome any ambiguity in legislation. The sustainable and predictable funding for this area of the regulator's work nevertheless remains an issue (see *Inputs* section for further discussion).

**The regulator has placed increasing emphasis on its consumer protection mandate in recent years with the liberalisation of the retail markets for electricity and gas**. The Portuguese sector now counts 29 retailers in the electricity sector and 12 in the retail gas market, in addition to the suppliers of last resort. The regulator has a team dedicated to handling consumer complaints and mediating disputes between operators and consumers, and has focused on providing clear, plain language information to better inform energy consumers of their rights. It provides funding and training to arbitration centres throughout the country that handle consumer complaints in the energy sector. It also provides training to the household consumer associations that sit on its consultative councils in order to build their capacity and ability to contribute to deliberations. Stakeholders recognise and appreciate ERSE's role in this regard. A recent survey commissioned by the regulator found that consumer support is seen as the area of ERSE's activities that has been growing the most. A planned internal restructuring of ERSE intends to bring together consumer protection-related functions to strengthen the regulator's work in this area even further.

### *Functions and powers*

**In general, ERSE has sufficient powers to carry out its functions, although there can be a time lag between gaining new responsibilities and the expansion of its enforcement powers.** ERSE's functions and powers include regulatory, advisory, mediation, supervisory and sanctioning (Table 1). The regulator currently lacks sanctioning powers in the wholesale energy, electric mobility and, to a lesser extent, the fuels sectors. The Energy Sector Sanctions Framework has not yet been updated to include electric mobility or the implementation of the EU Regulation on Wholesale Energy Market Integrity and Transparency ("REMIT"), while the latter gives ERSE supervisory responsibilities to monitor wholesale markets and investigate potential insider trading and market manipulation. ERSE is awaiting the transposition of EU directives into national legislation.

**ERSE's functions expand beyond national borders to cover the single electricity market with Spain, where it has advisory powers.** ERSE is part of the Council of Regulators of the Iberian Electricity Market (MIBEL), created by an international agreement between Spain and Portugal in 2004 to address issues in the development of the single electricity market. The MIBEL Council is composed of the Spanish regulatory authorities for securities (*Comisión Nacional del Mercado de Valores*, CNMV) and energy (*Comisión Nacional de los Mercados y la Competencia*, CNMC) and the corresponding entities in Portugal: CMVM (*Comissão do Mercado de Valores Mobiliários*) and ERSE. Market actors nevertheless raise concerns about insufficient regulatory alignment through MIBEL. Retail market regulations on either side of the border remain different, which can lead to different levels of business costs in the two countries. This can be challenging for cross-border market agents and can lead to different levels of consumer prices, impeding the functioning of a true single market. As the Council does not have executive power, its primary function is as a mechanism for information sharing. Draft regulation for the functioning of MIBEL, to be approved in Portugal or in Spain, are subject to the mandatory issuance of a non-binding co-ordinated statement of opinions by the Council.

### Table 1. ERSE's regulatory functions by sector

| Sector | Regulatory functions<br>ERSE is responsible for the preparation and approval of the following regulations: |
|---|---|
| Electricity | Regulation on Access to Networks and Interconnections<br>Regulation on Commercial Relations<br>Tariff Regulation<br>Regulation on Quality of Service<br>Regulation on Network Operations |
| Natural gas | Regulation on Access to Networks, Infrastructures and Interconnections<br>Regulation on Commercial Relations<br>Tariff Regulation<br>Regulation on Quality of Service<br>Regulation on Operation of Infrastructures |
| Fuels | Regulation of storage, collecting and exchanging LPG bottles<br>Regulation on market operators' compliance with the obligation to inform the consumer of petroleum fuels and LPG<br>Regulation on Commercial Relations for piped LPG<br>Regulation on Quality of Service for piped LPG<br>Tariff Regulation for piped LPG<br>Regulation on the Quality of Supply of Fuels |
| Electric mobility | Regulation on Electric Mobility |

Source: OECD Questionnaire, 2019.

*Recommendations:*

- **Advocate** for the expansion of appropriate sanctioning powers to REMIT, electric mobility and fuels sectors. ERSE could capitalise on its knowledge of forthcoming EU legislation through its involvement in ACER and other European organisations to engage proactively with the government on developing national legislation that grants ERSE appropriate powers in a timely manner**.**
- **Argue** for closer integration and harmonisation with Spain in the context of the Iberian market.
  - In the context of implementing the EU Clean Energy Package, particularly for retail-focused measures, ERSE could **identify** areas where it could take a common approach with CNMC to harmonise aspects of retail market regulation to facilitate market agents operating in both markets, to increase the level of competition and consumer benefits. Specific areas might include: regulations around smart metering, consumer information, billing requirements.
  - **Consider** establishing a cross-border consultative committee with representatives of industry, users and consumers on both sides of the border. This group could be tasked with identifying barriers to harmonisation and better outcomes for users/consumers and could be used as a sounding board for proposals and policies.

### *Strategic framework (vision, mission and objectives)*

**The regulator's strategic framework is embodied in a four-year plan that would be strengthened by more focus on desired outcomes.** ERSE operates within the framework of a four-year strategic plan (2019-2022) that sets objectives that span the regulator's different activities. The plan is defined in a participative manner including different technical teams and senior management at ERSE. The plan sets five strategic objectives and 27 associated priorities (Table 2). The objectives are phrased according to the different activities that ERSE carries out rather than the outcomes that ERSE seeks to achieve. Many of the objectives and priorities are an aggregate of several priorities and responsible parties, which will make it challenging to monitor and report on them. The plan does not include performance targets and indicators, missing an opportunity to use it to define ERSE as an outcome-focused regulatory authority and to use the plan for strategic steering of the regulator's activities and communicating on its performance. Recognising the value of such an approach, ERSE is working on defining indicators by strategic objective/priority (see section on *Output and Outcome* for further recommendations).

## Table 2. ERSE's strategic objectives analysed according to OECD input-process-output-outcome framework

| Strategic objectives | Priorities | Type of priority |
|---|---|---|
| 1. Fostering knowledge and the active participation of society in energy regulation and ensuring protection of the interests of present and future consumers | • To combat energy illiteracy by promoting the training and information to consumers and other stakeholders regarding the energy sector | OUTCOME/OUTPUT |
| | • To ensure consumer protection in an environment of innovation and development of new services | OUTCOME |
| | • To foster ERSE's external communication and adapt the contents according to the recipient | PROCESS |
| | • To innovate in the provision of relevant sector information | PROCESS |
| | • To strengthen public participation in regulatory decision-making | PROCESS |
| 2: Promoting efficient regulation of natural monopolies, in a context of decentralisation and innovation | • To assess impacts and strengthen the rationale of regulatory decisions | PROCESS |
| | • To promote the establishment of access to networks and infrastructure in a transparent, non-discriminatory way inducing overall efficiency (technical and commercial) | OUTCOME |
| | • To promote the setting of allowed revenues based on the economic sustainability of infrastructure and on the creation of added value for consumers, in a context of decentralisation and innovation | PROCESS |
| | • To promote economically efficient smart grids and related services, placing digitalisation at the disposal of consumers and society | OUTCOME |
| | • To promote an efficient tariff structure in a context of decentralisation and innovation | OUTPUT |
| | • To discuss methodologies for the regulation of natural monopolies with a view of their improvement in a context of decentralisation and innovation. | OUTPUT |
| 3: Improving the functioning of wholesale and retail energy markets, reinforcing trust and enabling consumer involvement | • To contribute to the harmonisation and integration of Iberian, regional and European energy markets | OUTCOME |
| | • To promote clear and unambiguous regulation (better regulatory definition) | PROCESS |
| | • To ensure a continuing supervision of the markets and the monitoring of regulatory obligations and consolidate sanctioning actions | PROCESS |
| | • To promote the efficiency of the markets and implement a risk management culture (guarantees) in the regulated sectors | OUTCOME & PROCESS |
| | • To foster consumers' active participation and demand management. | PROCESS |
| 4: Promoting clear, effective and dynamic regulation of natural monopolies, facilitating the energy transition | • To monitor compliance with legal and regulatory provisions, improving proximity actions for consumers and companies and their processes of reporting to ERSE. | PROCESS/OUTPUT |
| | • To promote a transparent, integrated and harmonised regulatory framework that ensures the complementarity of regulated sectors and a dynamic regulation through the development of pilot projects. | OUTPUT |
| | • To promote energy efficiency in all types of energy | OUTCOME |
| | • To identify, foresee and influence new trends and developments in the energy sector | OUTPUT |
| | • To envisage sanctioning actions in a context of energy transition and incorporate those challenges in our work | PROCESS |
| 5: Affirming ERSE's excellence | • To improve internal communications and knowledge exchange | INPUT |
| | • To promote ERSE's co-operation with similar entities and other national and international institutions | INPUT |
| | • To ensure the development of human resources, by promoting training and | INPUT |

| Strategic objectives | Priorities | Type of priority |
|---|---|---|
| | adaptation to new challenges | |
| | • Orientation towards a culture of planning and management, adopting control and monitoring tools for the activities carried out at ERSE | INPUT |
| | • Orientation towards a culture of information security and personal data protection | INPUT |
| | • Affirming ERSE's social concerns, namely in the involvement in social causes and in environmental sustainability. | PROCESS |

Notes: The OECD Framework for Regulatory Policy Evaluation uses an input-process-output-outcome logic, which breaks down the regulatory process into a sequence of discrete steps. The input-process-output-outcome logic is flexible and can be applied both to evaluate practices to improve regulatory policy in general, and also to evaluate regulatory policy in specific sectors, based on the identification of relevant strategic objectives.

Source: OECD analysis based on ERSE's strategic objectives 2019-2022, Strategic plan 2019-2022, ERSE, https://www.erse.pt/media/x23cbptt/plano-estrat%C3%A9gico-e-financeiro-plurianual-2019-2022.pdf.

**A more ambitiously and simply worded strategic framework would support ERSE's identity as a forward-looking regulatory authority**. The role of the regulator and its technical work are appreciated and understood by the regulated industry and other immediate stakeholders that sit on its consultative councils, but there is a lost opportunity with regard to projecting its vision and using its strategic framework to bring the message of its value to a wider audience (Figure 1). Moreover, ERSE's forward-looking work (such as its use of regulatory sandboxes), in addition to its ability to provide predictability and consumer protection, could be more clearly captured in the strategic framework. For example, while the regulator's strategic plan includes an analytical section on trends and challenges and the concepts of innovation and dynamic regulation appear among its strategic objectives, the vision and mission of the regulator do not articulate how ERSE fits into the "bigger picture" and contributes to driving progress in the energy sector.

## Figure 1. ERSE's vision and mission statements

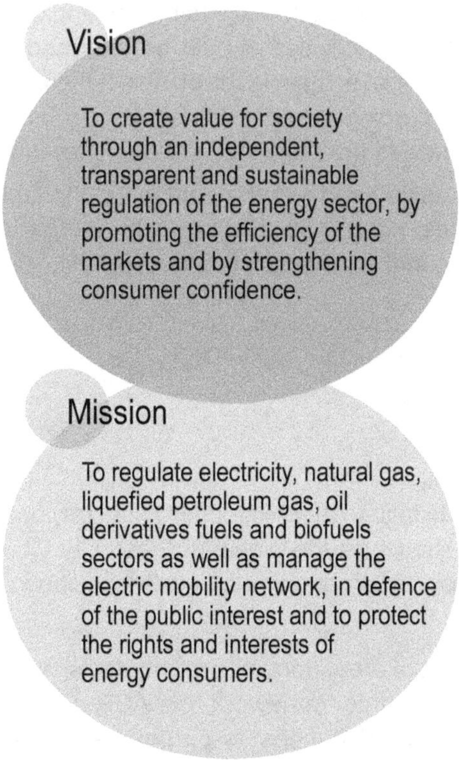

Vision

To create value for society through an independent, transparent and sustainable regulation of the energy sector, by promoting the efficiency of the markets and by strengthening consumer confidence.

Mission

To regulate electricity, natural gas, liquefied petroleum gas, oil derivatives fuels and biofuels sectors as well as manage the electric mobility network, in defence of the public interest and to protect the rights and interests of energy consumers.

Source: Strategic plan 2019-2022, ERSE, https://www.erse.pt/media/x23cbptt/plano-estrat%C3%A9gico-e-financeiro-plurianual-2019-2022.pdf.

*Recommendations*

- **Reinforce** the strategic framework of the regulator by introducing more outcome-focus and more accessible language at all levels (Box 1). This can be undertaken for the next strategic plan of the regulator, building on an assessment of the current one and lessons learnt, to be defined in a participative manner including internal teams and sector stakeholders.
  - **Phrase** high level elements of the strategic framework (vision, strategic objectives) as outcomes that ERSE will focus on delivering, rather than descriptions of ERSE activities.
  - **Devise** the "vision" as a statement of a desired future (10-20 year time horizon) and the "mission" as a statement of what the regulator does.
  - **Articulate** how ERSE fits into the 'bigger picture' and can contribute to driving the sector forward in a context of rapid change. Make explicit the link between the regulator's technical work and the value that this brings to the sector in terms that can be understood by a wide audience.
  - **Accompany** the strategic plan with clear, time-bound targets that can be monitored (see Box 2, and the Output and Outcomes section).
  - **Devise** and **implement** a communications strategy and plan for the vision and strategic framework of ERSE, with distinct activities and goals for internal and external stakeholders. The strategy will need a dedicated budget and resources for implementation.
  - **Publish** citizen's summaries or Q&As alongside ERSE reports, studies and regulatory codes, using simple and clear language to communicate on the regulator's activities to a wider non-technical audience.
- **Strengthen** ERSE's identity as a forward-looking regulatory authority by continuing to articulate its appetite for experimentation and flexibility, striving to push the frontiers.
  - **Carry out** a risk-appetite mapping to identify areas where the organisation is willing to take more risks (Box 3). OECD Best Practice Principles on Regulatory Enforcement and Inspections (OECD, 2014[1]) also provide guidance on assessing risk and developing regulatory responses. It advises that: all enforcement activities should be informed by the analysis of risks; each activity and business should have their level of risk assessed and enforcement resources should then be allocated accordingly; and, each set of regulations should likewise be given a level of priority commensurate to the risks they are trying to address.
  - **Continue developing** risk-taking and experimentation in the field of innovation, e.g. continued use of regulatory sandboxes, scaling up pilot projects, partnering with or increasing two-way conversations with industry on the process of innovation etc. (Box 4).

## Box 1. Vision statements and principles

### Australian Energy Regulator (AER)

The AER, and the other market bodies in the Australian energy sector, operate within a framework with an overarching statutory objective, known as the National Electricity Objective, which is to "promote efficient investment in, and efficient operation and use of, electricity services for the long term interests of consumers of electricity".

This objective is referenced at the start of most documents and decisions produced by the AER, and is widely known across the industry. Within this framework, the AER as an organisation, also sets out a purpose and strategic objectives. The AER defines its purpose as working towards making "energy consumers better off, now and in the future". The AER's strategic objectives and its regulatory activities are designed in a way to advance the regulator's purpose. This is explained in the strategic statement and in the annual corporate plan.

Source: Information provided by AER, 2020.

### Essential Services Commission of South Australia (ESCOSA)

ESCOSA has a long-term objective defined as "the protection of the long-term interests of South Australian consumers with respect to the price, quality and reliability of essential services", which is defined by legislation. On this, the regulator built its purpose statement of adding "long-term value to the South Australian community by meeting its objective through its independent, ethical and expert regulatory decisions and advice". In its strategy document, ESCOSA goes further and defines the values which will enable it achieve its statutory objective, and thus guide its regulatory activities: responsiveness, accountability, innovation, and the building of inclusive relationships.

Source: Information provided by ESCOSA, 2020.

### Financial Conduct Authority (FCA), United Kingdom

The FCA published in 2017 their Mission document, which is the framework within which the FCA takes strategic decisions, the reasoning behind the work undertaken, and the tools used to implement the regulation developed. Alongside an explanation of its regulatory remit within the scope of its three operational objectives, the FCA included in the Mission its decision-making framework which explains to the public how regulatory decisions are made within the remit of the FCA's objectives.

Furthermore, through the Mission, the FCA identified five types of harm and mapped these across its operational objectives. Each year, it reports in its Annual Report how its regulatory and enforcement tools were used to reduce and prevent this harm.

### Table 3. FCA Mission: types of harm for financial services consumers

| Type of harm | Relevant FCA operational objectives |
|---|---|
| Confidence and participation in markets are threatened by unacceptable conduct such as market abuse, unreliable performance or by disorderly failure | Market integrity<br>Consumer protection<br>Effective competition |
| Consumers buy unsuitable, or are mis-sold, products; poor customer service/treatment | Consumer protection<br>Effective competition |
| Important consumer needs are not met because of gaps in the existing range of products, consumer exclusion, lack of market resilience | Consumer protection<br>Effective competition |
| Prices too high or quality too low | Effective competition<br>Consumer protection |
| Risk of significant harmful side-effects on wider markets, the UK economy and wider society, e.g., crime/terrorism | Market integrity<br>Consumer protection |

Source: Financial Conduct Authority, Our Mission, 2017, https://www.fca.org.uk/publication/corporate/our-mission-2017.pdf.

## Box 2. The use of key performance indicators at the Brazilian Electricity Regulatory Agency (ANEEL)

ANEEL measures its performance using KPIs (or "strategic indicators"). These are linked to the strategic objectives which, in turn, are defined by ANEEL in its strategic planning or through legislation. A designated department (the Cabinet of the Director-General) is tasked with the monitoring of the performance indicators. Any ANEEL employee is able to consult at any time the performance of the indicators through a portal available on the intranet.

ANEEL has a total of 61 strategic indicators, linked to the 16 strategic objectives. Through the annual report, ANEEL provide an overview of its performance over time through the presentation of all strategic indicators and their comparison against the yearly targets.

The strategic indicators are categorised as follows, in order to cover all areas of the regulator:

- 7 strategic indicators for strategic objectives linked to **results**;
- 34 indicators for strategic objectives linked to **processes**; and
- 20 indicators for strategic objectives linked to **people and resources**.

Strategic indicators are designed to be all-encompassing, and to measure a wide range of aspects – both under the direct influence of the ANEEL, and the result of external factors. For instance, while ANEEL can directly impact the indicator on the timeliness of its regulatory decisions, the indicator on the average industry bond default rate is likely to be affected by matters outside ANEEL's direct control.

The performance of each indicator feeds directly into the assessment of the strategic objectives. Therefore, the composite score of each strategic objective is calculated based on the scores of the individual indicators.

This is a tangible means for ANEEL to firstly internally monitor progress towards achieving its strategic objectives through scoring of strategic indicators, which in turn are used by teams with the aim to translate the objectives into tangible (and measurable) targets, and secondly to provide accountability to stakeholders through the Annual Report.

Source: Information provided by ANEEL, 2020; ANEEL Annual Report, 2019, https://www.aneel.gov.br/documents/653889/14859944/Exerc%C3%ADcio+-+2019/b755a474-25e9-994d-7f00-c8a6ec8d8b86.

## Box 3. Risk Appetite Statement at Ireland's Commission for Regulation of Utilities (CRU)

Ireland's Commission for Regulation of Utilities (CRU) developed a Risk Appetite Statement to articulate the level and type of risk that the regulator will tolerate while delivering its mission and vision. The statement forms a key component of the organisation's Risk Management Framework.

The statement is intended to act as a guide to management indicating:

- The areas where compliance is key and a risk averse approach is necessary;
- The areas where innovation is encouraged; and
- How the regulator balances risk and opportunity in pursuit of value.

The main purpose of the Risk Management Framework is to integrate the process for managing risk into the organisation's various governance and operational processes. These include strategy and planning, management, reporting, policy development, and values and culture.

As part of the Risk Management Framework, the CRU has developed as Risk Appetite Statement, which states that the CRU overall has a conservative risk appetite. The CRU acts in accordance with this Risk Appetite Statement to achieve its strategic objectives. The CRU recognizes that it is not practical or desirable to avoid all risk. Accordingly, the CRU tolerates some risk, in pursuit of its mission and values. Acceptance of any risk is subject to ensuring that potential benefits and risks are fully understood and that measures to mitigate risks have been established. The Risk Appetite Statement establishes risks in a number of categories, and the CRU have considered a number of factors to determine its tolerance for each of these risks. The risk categories considered by the CRU are:

- Reputation
- Legal and compliance
- Financial
- Strategy / project
- Policy Formulation
- Operational
- Technology
- Personnel / Talent Management
- External
- Stakeholder and Communications

The Risk Appetite Statement is intended to be a living document. CRU reviews its risk appetite tolerances annually to reflect changes in the external environment.

Source: Information provided by CRU, 2020.

## Box 4. Energy Regulation Sandbox at UK's energy regulator, Ofgem

Ofgem launched in July 2020 their refreshed Energy Regulation Sandbox. This follows from the 2017 experience, when Ofgem worked with 68 innovators from the energy sector recruited through two sandbox application windows. Ofgem analysed the results of these sandbox cohorts, and published a report on *Insights from running the regulatory sandbox*. This not only provided the regulator with valuable insight on how to adapt the future Sandbox programmes, but also provided public accountability and gave future applicants further understanding of the process.

The Sandbox service complements current Ofgem reforms by allowing innovators to trial or launch new products, services, methodologies and business models without some of the usual rules applying. These can be rules that Ofgem controls (usually in licences) or, in some circumstances, from the rulebooks (codes) owned by industry, which underpin the day-to-day operations of the energy system. The Sandbox offers a range of tools to innovators across all the regulated areas, including suppliers, generators and network companies, or even those who are not directly regulated by Ofgem – for example third party intermediaries and energy services providers.

The use of Sandboxes in 2020 is considered an ideal time, as the energy system and consumer behaviour are evolving. As well as responding to the long term challenge of achieving net-zero, the Sandbox can help innovators and industry participants respond to nearer term challenges wrought by COVID-19, with consumer demand patterns changing as more people work from home, and more reliance on renewable generation due to lower levels of industrial demand.

The Energy Regulation Sandbox is run by the Ofgem's dedicated Innovation Link team, which offers support on energy regulation to businesses looking to launch new products, services or business models and will act as the single point of entry for innovators who also wish to access the flexibility available in industry codes that have developed sandbox capabilities.

Source: Information provided by Ofgem, 2020.

### *Co-ordination*

**There are no permanent, sector-wide mechanisms for co-ordination between different actors in the Portuguese energy sector.** However, the government establishes *ad hoc* groups that appear to work well. The ministry in in charge of the energy sector (Ministry of the Environment and Climate Action, *Ministério do Ambiente e da Ação Climática* (MAAC)) establishes working or expert groups on specific topics depending on need. ERSE participates upon invitation in such working groups.

**ERSE counts on three independent consultative councils that in many ways play a significant role in supporting co-ordination between stakeholders from public authorities (including MAAC), consumer associations and industry.** Although the councils' primary purpose is to provide a consultation forum on the regulator's decisions, they serve a secondary, indirect purpose of enabling multilateral discussions between the major players in the sector, as opposed to a one-way or bilateral consultation process between the regulator and its stakeholders. This is a source of great value to Portugal's energy sector as it enables players to understand each other's perspectives and develop relationships of trust over time. In this way, the councils provide stability to stakeholders and achieve consensus in their statements in an impressive 90% of cases.

**ERSE is clear on its role and responsibilities vis-à-vis other actors in the sector and has taken proactive measures to address challenges of co-ordination when needed, but the division of responsibilities between entities is not always clear for regulated industry or the public.** ERSE co-ordinates with a large number of organisations at national and international levels. The regulator is explicitly empowered and required through its statutes to co-operate with other bodies where this will assist in meeting common objectives. To overcome cases of ambiguity in responsibilities, ERSE has also established a number of co-operation agreements. Nevertheless, resolving overlaps often requires clarification on a case-by-case basis. ERSE has on occasion proposed new legislation when it has identified gaps or overlaps in responsibilities and maintains a record of institutions with whom it shares joint competences. While legislation defines the obligations for co-ordination between ERSE and other public agencies for providing non-binding opinions (e.g. with the Competition Authority, AdC) there are no mechanisms in place to ensure broader aspects of co-ordination such as information sharing. Moreover, the recent reorganisation of regulatory functions between ERSE, the Directorate General for Energy and Geology (DGEG) and ENSE appears to have sown confusion and the new division of responsibilities appears to be unclear.

**The area of consumer protection requires particularly careful co-ordination given the large number of entities involved in handling complaints.** Several organisations are potentially involved, including ERSE, ENSE, the Directorate-General for Consumer-Affairs, DECO (a private consumer rights association), the Economic and Food Safety Authority (ASAE) as well as nine independent arbitration centres. Most of the arbitration centres serve a particular region and they are not specialised in the energy sector; they cover all economic sectors and can only process complaints from households and not, for example, small businesses. Seven of the centres are partly financed[2] by and receive training from ERSE. There is also disparity in type of mandate between different institutions involved in consumer protection: for example, the decisions of the arbitration centres are binding, unlike ERSE, which does not have the power to impose a resolution to a dispute. The large number of organisations involved could reduce consistency and predictability in decisions towards market agents, if each organisation follows different processes or interprets and applies rules differently. The system could also create risk to consumer harm as consumers may be confused or intimidated by the complex or unclear processes to bring a claim.

*Recommendations*

- **Assess** which areas of work could benefit from having formal co-ordination mechanisms in place:
  - **Consider establishing** a formal co-ordination mechanism with the Competition Authority (AdC) that includes provisions for information-sharing. The co-operation agreement could cover points such as data ownership, what the information can be used for and for how long, and who has the duty to act on information that points to harm on competition, etc.
  - **Invest** in developing a strong understanding of the different operational roles of ERSE, ENSE and DGEG. This could be aided by simple solutions, such as using the same text on all three websites, to producing more detailed information, such as publishing an "approach to supervision" document to explain to the markets the current division of responsibilities within the sector, what types of entities can expect ERSE visits, and what ERSE will look at. Establishing a "one-stop shop" for data collection and administrative processes could also ease regulatory burden.
- **Advocate** for an assessment of the effectiveness of the current consumer complaints system for the energy sector. The assessment could be mandated jointly by concerned public bodies and carried out by an external party. Such an assessment could investigate, for example, if all actors (households, small businesses, large businesses, etc.) have access to proportionate and specialised support in case of a complaint, if information on processes is made clearly available, if decisions are consistent across authorities and the country. If relevant and applicable, the conclusions of such an assessment could be used to rehaul, align or consolidate practices and mechanisms in the interest of all consumers in the energy sector (Box 5).

### Box 5. CRU's role in customer complaint resolution

Ireland's Commission for Regulation of Utilities (CRU) has responsibility for customer complaint resolution in the energy and water sectors.

The Commission has a statutory obligation (defined in legislation) to provide a complaint resolution service to domestic and small and medium business customers who have an unresolved complaint with their energy supplier or network operator. Only customers who have completed their supplier or network operator's complaint resolution process, and failed to reach a resolution, may raise their complaint with the Commission.

CRU has the power to direct suppliers/network operators to resolve a complaint in a particular fashion. For example, the Commission can issue determinations and directions to suppliers and network operators, including the payment of a refund or compensation, where appropriate.

Final decisions are not subject to appeal and are binding on the energy supplier/network operator. However, customers are not obliged to accept the Commission's findings and are free to take the matter further in another forum if they wish to do so.

CRU has a team of 5-6 staff dedicated to this function that is also responsible for reporting and consumer survey work.

Having responsibility for complaints resolution enables CRU to have visibility of the issues in the sector that can then inform the regulator's decisions on whether to update its regulations in response. Having a single organisation interpreting and making decisions on the compliance of energy companies with regulations also increases regulatory predictability, reduces complexity in the system and simplifies the process for consumers.

Source: Information provided by CRU, 2020.

### *Input into policy making and relations with the executive and legislative branches*

**Given its strong technical capacity and expertise, ERSE opinions carry weight and are valued by the executive.** ERSE has a formal advisory role and contributes to policy development through the provision of advice, non-binding opinions, studies and participation in working groups. The time that ERSE has to comply with requests can vary from a few days for the more informal requests to a month for formal requests. Its opinions to formal requests are made public via its website and in its annual report to ensure transparency. ERSE estimates that contributing to the formulation and refinement of policies, laws and regulations consumes about 10% to 15% of its total resources, mostly staff time. The regulator reports that this is manageable, although the burden can be considerable if several requests are received at the same time.

**Transparent reporting and approval processes are in place but dialogue between ERSE, the executive and the parliament could be improved.** The government defines the broad energy policy within which ERSE must act as an independent regulatory body. The government and parliament also approve the regulator's annual budget and the respective multiannual plan, its balance sheet, and the annual report and accounts. Without prejudice to its functional independence, ERSE must keep the government informed of its regulatory activity, reporting on recommendations, legislative proposals and draft external regulations which it intends to adopt, as well as on instruments in the framework of the government's general policy for regulated sectors.[3] ERSE informs the member of the government responsible for energy in writing about the launch of public consultations, the submission of the tariff proposal, as well as of the approval of the tariff regulation and tariff decisions. However, beyond this there appear to be few institutionalised processes, such as a statement of expectations, to ensure close and effective dialogue between the regulator and the ministry in charge of energy (Ministry of the Environment and Climate Action, MAAC). Furthermore, on occasion the regulator has been taken by surprise by additional tasks or responsibilities included in the annual state budget, on which there has been no prior dialogue with or warning from the executive or the legislative.

#### *Recommendations*

- **Take steps** to build a constructive, 'no surprises' relationship with the executive and legislative:
  - **Set up** a formalised and structured dialogue with the executive for each year. The objective of such a dialogue could help set expectations of work priorities and deliverables.
  - **Request** that MAAC send ERSE a letter during the preparation of the annual state budget that would highlight any new responsibilities that deviate from the approved multi-annual plan. ERSE could formally respond before the finalisation of the annual state budget.

- **Advocate** for the creation of a policy initiatives forum hosted by government that convenes relevant authorities intervening in the energy sector (e.g. MAAC, DGEG, ERSE, ENSE…) to share planned policy changes, legislative changes or major supervisory actions (Box 6).

### Box 6. Regulatory Initiatives Forum and Grid for the UK's financial sector

The Financial Services Regulatory Initiatives Forum is formed of the main five institutions which impact the financial services sector (Financial Conduct Authority, Bank of England, Prudential, Regulation Authority, Payment Systems Regulator, Competition and Markets Authority), plus the HM Treasury (government department) as observer member.

The Forum's role is to improve information-sharing on the timing and operational impact of regulatory initiatives. The goal is to help manage the operational impact on firms from implementing these initiatives. The Forum is a mechanism for sharing information and supporting coordination between authorities – focusing on the timing of regulatory initiatives. The content of regulation remains the responsibility of individual Forum members. Reflecting this, the Forum itself does not have decision-making powers.

The public outcome of the work of the Forum is the Regulatory Initiatives Grid, which is published every 6 months, and which sets out the planned regulatory workplan over the following twelve months. It will help firms and other stakeholders understand – and plan for – the timing of the initiatives that may have a significant operational impact on them.

At the moment, the Grid is run as a 1-year pilot, and the Forum encourages industry and stakeholders to engage with it and provide feedbacks, so that its content and format can be amended so that it becomes as useful as possible for its users.

Source: Financial Conduct Authority, Regulatory Initiatives Forum, 2020, https://www.fca.org.uk/publications/corporate-documents/regulatory-initiatives-grid 2020; Financial Conduct Authority, Regulatory Initiatives Grid, 2020, https://www.fca.org.uk/news/press-releases/financial-services-regulatory-initiatives-forum-launches-grid.

### *Independence*

**ERSE performs well on several dimensions of independence and has policies in place to foster a culture of independence internally. Nevertheless, it has been facing restrictions on its autonomy over financial and human resources.** ERSE shows arrangements closest to good practice on independence[4] among energy regulators in OECD countries as per the *OECD Indicators on the Governance of Sector Regulators* (Figure 2). The regulator also demonstrates independence in its technical decision-making, drawing on empirical evidence and transparent stakeholder input. The Board and Heads of Division and similar managers (ERSE senior management) provide independent leadership bolstered by post-separation employment policies such as a two-year cooling off period during which they cannot work in the regulated industry. During this period, Board members are compensated. Staff, however, do not have any post-employment restrictions. ERSE statutes, internal codes and plans also include provisions that deal with ethics, corruption prevention, incompatibilities and conflicts of interests. With regard to regulator resources, despite legislation that establishes the regulator's *de jure* independence, provisions introduced through the annual state budgets have restricted ERSE's autonomy in managing its financial and human resources in recent years (see *Input* section for more detailed assessment and recommendations).

Figure 2. ERSE demonstrates strong independence

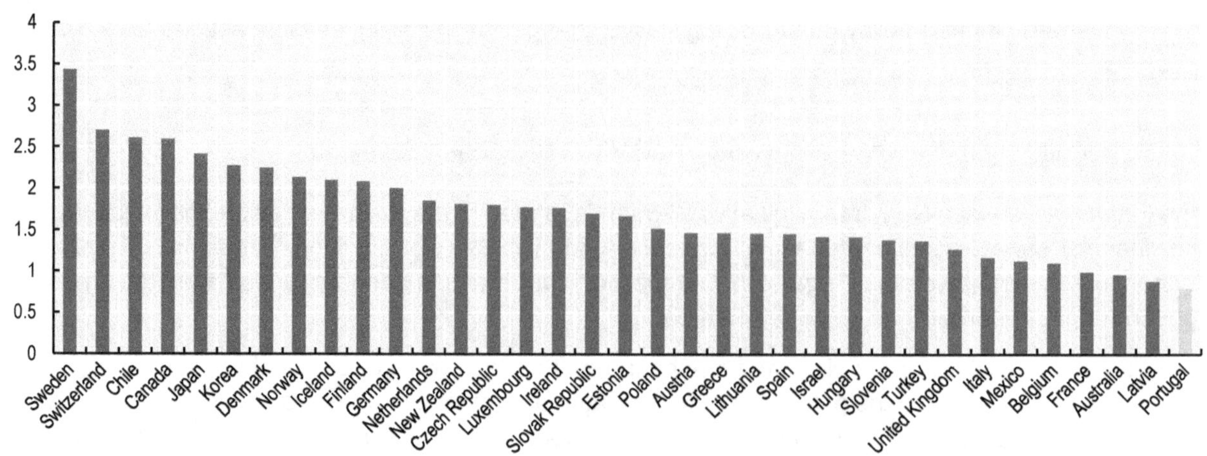


1. Scores are on a scale from zero (most effective governance arrangement) to six (least effective governance arrangement).
2. The independence component maps the degree to which a regulator operates independently and with no undue influence from both the political power and the regulated sectors. Questions are organised into three subsections: relationship with the executive, staff and budget. It seeks to measure aspects of *de facto* independence through a variety of dimensions beyond only *de jure* independence.
Source: OECD (2018), Database on the Governance of Sector Regulators.

*Recommendation:*

- **Establish** an association or group of Portuguese independent regulatory authorities as a forum to discuss common challenges and opportunities and advance common positions when necessary (akin to the French "*Club de Régulateurs*"). This group could be used, for example, to discuss restrictions to financial and management autonomy faced by all Portuguese regulators.

## Input

**ERSE is funded mostly by regulatory contributions from industry, and not by the government budget, providing a solid underpinning for the regulator's financial independence.** The vast majority (95%) of ERSE's income comes from contributions (fees) paid by concession holders of the electricity and gas transmission networks,[5] which are included in the network access tariffs paid by consumers (Table 4). The fees are defined by ERSE according to criteria set out in legislation. Since the expansion of the regulator's responsibilities in 2018, ERSE also receives a small proportion of its revenue from fees paid by market agents in the fuels sector (2% in 2019, and 1.4% in 2020). ERSE's finances are well managed; the external auditor's reports indicate that ERSE follows sound financial management and budgeting practices and do not signal any major financial risks.

**The regulator reports to have sufficient resources to meet most of its objectives although there is uncertainty in the funding for its fuels sector work.** ERSE's income has risen by 16% over the last three years, driven by contributions from the natural gas sector and new resources from the fuels sector. However, the regulator deems that the resources for the fuels sector work are insufficient. Furthermore, ERSE lacks budgetary autonomy and long-term certainty on this portion of its income. The government determines the amount of fees due from fuel sector actors according to a formula that it sets on an annual basis. This creates a degree of uncertainty on ERSE's regulatory and financial autonomy and difficulties to plan beyond the current financial year for these activities. Although the fuels work represents a small proportion of ERSE's overall budget, the current system for setting fees undermines the regulator's financial independence.

## Table 4. ERSE sources of revenue

2016-19

| Source of revenue | 2016 | | 2017 | | 2018 | | 2019 | |
|---|---|---|---|---|---|---|---|---|
| | Amount | % of total funding | Amount | % of total funding | Amount | % of total funding | Amount | % of total funding |
| Contributions (Electricity) | 6 428 420 | 65 | 6 228 287 | 64 | 6 434 796 | 60 | 6 632 563 | 58 |
| Contributions (Gas) | 3 311 610 | 33 | 3 503 412 | 36 | 3 779 166 | 35 | 4 421 709 | 39 |
| Contributions (Oil) | 0 | 0 | 0 | 0 | 0 | 0 | 239 828 | 2 |
| Fines | 113 000 | 1 | 32 920 | 0 | 422 230 | 4 | 188 053 | 2 |
| Interest | 11 436 | 0 | 0 | 0 | 0 | 0 | 0 | 0 |
| EU Institutions (SAMA) | 45 739 | 1 | | 0 | 0 | 0 | 0 | 0 |
| Others | 6 347 | 0 | 8 853 | 0 | 36 858 | 0 | 4 726 | 0 |
| TOTAL | 9 916 552 | 100 | 9 773 472 | 100 | 10 673 050 | 100 | 11 486 879 | 100 |

Source: Information provided by ERSE, 2020.

**In terms of human resources, ERSE benefits from an experienced, knowledgeable and technically proficient staff that is highly committed to the organisation. A new generation of staff recently recruited can bring in fresh ideas and perspectives as ERSE looks to the future.** As of December 2019, ERSE employs 95 staff, 80% of which are professional staff, which is generally felt to correspond to the workload of the regulator. Stakeholders regard ERSE staff as technically highly competent. The most represented fields in ERSE are engineering (24%), law (22%) and economics (22%). Over a quarter of staff (26%) have been with ERSE since its founding (ERSE Annual Report, 2018), while 27% have been at the organisation less than three years. The coexistence of different "generations" of staff within the regulator may create challenges in terms of creating a cohesive "ERSE culture" but is an opportunity to bring in new ideas and ways of working and to position ERSE as a forward-looking regulator.

**Lengthy processes for recruitment due to the need for government authorisation may reduce the regulator's agility in bringing in new skills.** Looking ahead, ERSE highlights the need to strengthen its capabilities in emerging fields (such as the energy transition, energy systems integration, energy communities, and circular economy), communication and support to market actors, behavioural science and data analytics. Since 2012, due to rules encompassing the Portuguese public administration, the regulator must request government authorisation to increase its headcount. As the approval process can take up to a year, this adds significant time to bring new staff on board and may reduce the agility of the regulator.

**This restriction is symptomatic of a broader climate of constraints on ERSE's HR and budgetary autonomy since the 2009 financial crisis.** Portugal was deeply affected by the crisis, leading to an international bailout package and a period of intense austerity policies that affected the whole Portuguese public administration and independent regulators alike. Although ERSE's budgetary autonomy is enshrined in its statues and in the Framework Law of Independent Administrative Entities, subsequent legislation introduced through the annual state budgets as a result of austerity policies curtailed ERSE's autonomy in managing its resources to a certain degree. The restrictions apply to all public sector bodies including independent regulatory authorities in Portugal, although the latter are not funded by government budget. Some of these restrictions have been lifted in the last year or so, while others have been added more recently despite the general easing of austerity policies in line with Portugal's economic recovery. Examples include:

- In some instances, a portion of the approved budget not being released and unable to be spent without prior authorisation from the government body responsible for finance.

- The government seeking to retain ERSE's budget surplus for the state budget, rather than it being returned to energy consumers through the tariffs, as is foreseen in law.[6]
- Limits on public procurement spending were introduced in the 2019 state budget, and had been included on occasion in previous state budgets.
- Authorisation needed for the addition of new budget lines to ERSE's annual budget, even those related to core functions of the regulator (e.g. for audits).
- Salary cuts in 2009 and a freeze on salaries between 2009 and 2020.
- Elimination of performance-related bonuses.
- Government approval needed for promotions (restriction removed in 2020).

**Despite some restrictions, a level of autonomy in its management of human resources has allowed ERSE to weather this difficult period relatively well in terms of staff retention.** Staff turnover averaged 4% between 2016 and 2019. The ability of ERSE to set its own salaries outside of public servant bands gives the regulator significant potential to attract and retain talent.[7] Salaries at entry level are competitive compared to the Portuguese energy sector, becoming less so at senior levels. A higher turnover rate at senior management level (11% between 2016 and 2019) could be a reflection of this difference. ERSE also compensated for the inability to reward good performance with promotions and bonuses by offering other incentives, such as opportunities for training.

**While restrictions appear to be easing, readiness for similar measures in the future is important given current economic forecasts.** In a positive development, some of the budget restrictions that were in place in 2019 have been removed in the most recent state budget. Although it appears that austerity measures may be easing, the limitations that were imposed on regulators' financial independence set a precedent. At the time of writing, the prospect of another recession following the novel coronavirus pandemic seems possible. It is conceivable that a government could introduce similar austerity measures in the future. ERSE's experience of the post-2009 period could provide valuable lessons for how to respond should the situation be repeated.

*Recommendations:*

- **Advocate** for lifting of certain practices that limit the financial autonomy of the regulator and anticipate future challenges in post-COVID economy and effects on public finances. The regulator should contact the executive as part of a proactive stance to address practices highlighted the paragraphs above, and safeguard its HR & budgetary autonomy in case of future austerity measures. As part of this strategy, ERSE could:
  - **Strengthen** direct engagement with the ministry in charge of finance on ERSE's annual budget and activity plan ahead of their official submission for approval.
  - **Collect** information on the impact of the current and any foreseen restrictions on its ability to carry out its tasks effectively, and appraise the practical implications of this upon the sector and consumers;
  - **Advocate** for setting fees for the fuel sector on a longer-term basis, with criteria set in legislation;
  - **Explain** how ERSE delivers value for money (VFM), maximising the delivery of its objectives whilst minimising cost. For example, show how ERSE has embedded VFM criteria such as efficiency and effectiveness into the culture of the organisation (e.g. through the efficient use of cross-sector teams) and how a VFM strategy is taken into account throughout the decision-making process.

  - **Work with** other economic regulators and influential figures within the energy sector to publicly advocate for the importance and value of independent economic regulation and develop common positions;
  - **Proactively communicate** to key stakeholders such as parliamentarians the value of independent economic regulation jointly with other regulators as a pre-emptive strategy in case of future challenges to financial independence.
- **Encourage** mobility of junior-to-mid level staff generally in the energy sector and other public bodies in Portugal and abroad, including in other regulatory agencies, as part of an overall drive to promote innovation (Box 7). Staff mobility could ensure a stream of fresh knowledge and ideas and a greater diversity of perspectives. This could be achieved through secondments or temporary placements as part of a professional development programme. Encouraging mobility is particularly important in the context of a relatively small country such as Portugal. ERSE may need to advocate for the removal of legal obstacles to recruitment or secondment from other parts of the energy sector (public or private) or secondments from other bodies.
- **Ensure** that ERSE remains an attractive place to work and strengthen the culture of meritocracy, enhancing visibility and opportunities including for junior-to-mid level staff.
- **Develop** a range of internal career options including non-management posts for specialised staff who do not wish to pursue management responsibilities.
- **Expand** the system of opportunities for staff development such as training, publishing or presenting at conferences.
- **Collect** data on salaries in the regulated sectors and other Portuguese regulators to enable benchmarking and ensure ERSE salaries remain competitive with comparable agencies, particularly at senior levels.
- **Harness** the performance evaluation system to reward good performance with career progression, complementing the incentives that are already in place such as training opportunities.
- **Encourage** staff mobility within the regulator, taking the opportunity of the restructuring as a first step. For example, ERSE could carry out a 'call for interest' exercise so that staff can indicate if they are interested in moving teams. A more formalised mobility programme could be envisaged for the medium-to-long term. In general, ERSE could advertise all openings (internal and external) to all staff.
- **Implement** measures to bring together different "generations" of ERSE staff, in the interest of institutional culture and ownership for the values and strategic framework of the regulator. Concrete measures could include "buddy-up" programmes or mentorship schemes between long-standing members of staff and more recent recruits.

### Box 7. International secondment arrangements at the Australian Competition and Consumer Commission (ACCC) and the Australian Energy Regulator (AER)

The ACCC and the AER see value in secondments as a tool for staff development and capacity building (enhancing knowledge, skills and experience) and for building understanding and closer relationships with peer and partner agencies and stakeholders. The ACCC/AER has a number of formal and informal secondment arrangements in place for staff at different levels including the following:

- The ACCC has established a number of reciprocal secondment arrangements with other government agencies, including the Treasury and the Department of Communications. To deepen understanding and knowledge of the indigenous peoples of Australia, the ACCC has a formal arrangement for placement of selected staff in an indigenous community for six months. The ACCC also has secondment arrangements in places with its peer agency in New Zealand (the New Zealand Commerce Commission, NZCC). The current Chief Economist of the NZCC is on leave from the ACCC. The ACCC also hosts staff from other agencies from time to time, such as staff on secondment from the United States Consumer Product Safety Commission.

- The ACCC (together with the New Zealand Commerce Commission) has a formal training and secondment programme to assist ASEAN countries as they seek to implement competition laws and to combat anti-competitive activities. This programme includes staff exchanges, expert placements, secondments and resident advisors between ASEAN countries and the ACCC/NZCC. Secondments and exchanges have occurred with the competition authorities of Singapore, Malaysia, Viet Nam, Laos, Myanmar and Indonesia, amongst others. ACCC Chief Operating Officer Rayne de Gruchy commented "CLIP activities, such as staff exchanges, are proving an effective way to share know-how among agencies, as well as developing mutual understanding and relationships that can help agencies become operational more quickly."
- At the more senior level, the ACCC has an arrangement for exchange of senior management with the Canadian Competition Bureau. The Chair of the ACCC, Rod Sims, has said about this arrangement: "Exchange programmes like this allow the ACCC to build partnerships with international counterpart agencies to share and develop knowledge. These relationships are particularly valuable when it comes to pursuing cross-border investigations".
- Similarly, the AER makes use of secondments to keep up to date with regulatory best practice and to build technical knowledge. The AER has organised staff exchanges with AEMO (the electricity system operator in Australia) and with a few international energy regulators. The AER has a formal staff exchange / secondment arrangement with Ofgem in the UK. Several AER staff have spent between 6-12 months at Ofgem. The AER has hosted several staff from Ofgem in return. The AER also has an exchange programme with IESO (the system operator in the state of Ontario in Canada), as part of an arrangement between the members of the Energy Intermarket Surveillance Group (EISG), the peak international group coordinating and sharing skills between energy market surveillance and enforcement bodies.

The ACCC/AER has developed a secondment policy covering the various practical and legal issues associated with secondments. As a general rule, when a secondment opportunity becomes available the opportunity is advertised to all staff along with the selection criteria and selection process. On the whole the ACCC/AER considers that secondments provide valuable opportunities for staff development and building understanding and co-operation across agencies.

Source: Information provided by ACCC/AER, 2020.

## Process

### *Governing body and decision making*

**ERSE's three-person Board of Directors is selected through a transparent process that provides safeguards for independence**. The board comprises a president and two members. Legislation establishes that board members must have adequate qualifications, recognised independence and technical and professional competence in the regulated activities. Of the three current board members, two were former ERSE staff and one was formerly the ERSE Tariff Council president. Board members are appointed by the Council of Ministers, following their nomination by the member of government responsible for energy and opinions from an independent appointments committee (CRESAP, the Public Administration Recruitment and Selection Committee) and the parliament. Although the opinion of the parliamentary commission is not binding, it appears to be a robust check on power: the appointment of a candidate to the board was once rejected following a negative opinion from the parliament.

**A longer time required between Board appointments could support continuity and decouple the process from political cycles**. Members are appointed for a term of six years, non-renewable, and appointments must be staggered, with a minimum period of six months between appointments. This provision opens the possibility for an entirely new board to be in place within a little over a year, which could undermine continuity in the regulator's strategic direction and predictability in decision-making.

**The board's wide-ranging responsibilities and small size may reduce its capacity to focus on strategic matters**. The Board's vast responsibilities combine both strategic and executive functions, which is not unusual in the Portuguese context and in smaller regulatory authorities in other jurisdictions. Board members act as members of the senior management team rather than being at arm's length from the operations of the regulator. The absence of the Director-General for Regulation post since 2017 or another executive management position results in the board engaging directly with heads of Division without the support of an intermediate level. The board has agreed a division of labour whereby each member oversees the work of particular divisions, and all divisions and offices report directly to the board. Board members are highly involved in the work of their assigned divisions. The board holds a weekly co-ordination meeting with all heads of division and each member meets weekly with their assigned divisions. This may undermine the Board's ability to dedicate time to strategic, foresight activities.

**Decision-making appears to be a highly efficient process supported by a digital tool that ensures internal transparency. External transparency mechanisms are more limited.** Board meetings take place once a week and are preceded by an informal meeting during which members discuss issues and prepare for the formal meeting. The board uses a digital platform ("Portal do CA") to manage the decision-making process, through which ERSE teams submit relevant items for approval, information or review. All exchanges within the decision-making process are recorded in the portal, although in practice board members will usually have discussed issues in person with the relevant head of division in the course of their regular meetings with teams. Decisions are taken by majority or by unanimous decision of the three board members. The president has the deciding vote. When the board takes a decision, the relevant head of division/manager is notified automatically through the portal. ERSE publishes the non-confidential versions of its decisions, sends them to its mailing list and may publish them on its website. ERSE does not publish the minutes of the board meetings.

**Decisions are informed by internal and external inputs; external inputs provide valuable information and perspective that ERSE uses in its decision making**. The board relies greatly on the technical input from ERSE teams and in particular the heads of division. Three independent, external bodies (the Advisory Council, the Tariff Council and the Fuels Council) provide non-binding opinions on all proposed regulatory decisions and also on corporate documents, such as the annual budget, in the case of the Advisory Council (see section on *Engagement*). The board places great importance on the opinions of the councils, which provides an important challenge function in the decision-making process.

*Recommendations:*

- **Invest in** the Board's strategic, outward-looking role, dedicating more time to monitoring future challenges and opportunities in the industry; continuing to foster constructive, cordial relationships with the executive and the parliament; and representing the organisation externally with aligned messaging.
- **Alleviate** the Board from certain operational and management decisions, in order to free time for its strategy and policy setting duties.
    - **Look for** further opportunities to delegate decision-making. For example, create an executive position (e.g. COO) or assign the reinstated DG Regulation with responsibilities for operational and management decisions (e.g. performance evaluations, training and leave plans

compliance, occupational health and safety, risk management, approving expenditure above certain thresholds…).

  - **Rotate** responsibility of divisions and areas of work among board members.

- **Advocate** increasing the minimum time required between board appointments from six months to at least one year.
- **Introduce** mechanisms to improve the transparency of the board's decision-making to all stakeholders. For example, the board could publish summaries of its meetings, redacting any confidential or commercially sensitive information (Box 8).

### Box 8. Transparency of decision-making

Regulators have developed a number of tools in order to ensure transparency and accountability towards the industry.

**Ireland's Commission for Regulation of Utilities (CRU)**

Prior to 2020, Ireland's Commission for Regulation of Utilities (CRU) did not publish the minutes of its commission meetings. In response to a request for the minutes under Freedom of Information (FOI), the CRU reconsidered this approach, in light of its commitment to transparency in its decision-making. Following this review, the CRU has now started publishing the minutes of its weekly Commission meetings.

Source: CRU, 2020.

**Brazil's Electricity Regulatory Agency (ANEEL)**

Brazil's Electricity Regulatory Agency (ANEEL) has in place a number of measures aimed at promoting transparency of regulatory decision-making.

***Board meetings***

Agendas for board meetings are published at least 5 days in advance on ANEEL's website. The public can attend a board meeting in person or watch a live-stream on ANEEL's website. For each board decision, the act along with information about the vote and supporting documents are published in the Federal Official Gazette (*Diário Oficial da União*) and on ANEEL's website. In addition, the video recordings of the board meetings are uploaded to ANEEL's YouTube channel, so they can be consulted retrospectively by anyone.

***Official meetings***

Summaries of other non-confidential official meetings are published regularly on ANEEL's website.

Source: Information provided by ANEEL, 2020.

### *Internal organisation and management*

**ERSE's internal teams are organised by function rather than by sector, a feature that appears to give the regulator a certain degree of agility as it has taken on responsibilities for new sectors over the years.** Such a structure may also help in terms of ensuring consistency of regulatory processes across sectors. The current exception is a small team that was created to work on ERSE's new duties in the fuel sector, an 'internal commission' of four people (the National Petroleum System Installation Commission, CISPN).

**A long restructuring process runs the risk of slowing down the implementation of activities and creates uncertainty for staff.** ERSE is currently restructuring, a process that was scheduled to finish in 2020. The rationale of the restructuring is multi-faceted: to consolidate the consumer protection activities that are dispersed across different teams, to strengthen focus on particular areas (e.g. on innovation through an 'Innovation and special projects' office or on internal procedures with the 'internal management' office) and to create intermediate management positions within the divisions. The organisation by function rather than sector will continue under the new structure. Staff report that certain activities have slowed down in anticipation of the definitive implementation of the reorganisation. The lengthy process also appears to be creating some uncertainty among staff and runs the risk of instilling 'reform fatigue'.

**The recent expansion of the workforce may test the limits of internal processes that worked well previously.** The regulator has grown significantly in recent years. Between 2016 and 2019, ERSE's workforce increased by over 20% to 95 staff. Some internal processes that may require co-ordination between different teams (e.g. making requests for data to regulated entities) seem to rely on informal contacts and understanding between staff rather than codified processes or policies. This approach may have been adequate at a smaller scale and with a core of staff with long-standing working relationships. It may not be as effective in a larger organisation with a significant number of new staff. As the 2018 annual report shows, 27% of staff have been at the organisation less than three years. The second largest cohort at 26% is those that have been with ERSE since its founding. As part of the on-going restructuring, ERSE intends to create a team whose terms of reference will include improving the coherence of internal processes (the Unit for Internal Management). This team will play an important role in finding workable solutions to this challenge.

*Recommendations:*

- **Embed** institutional renewal in the internal restructuring process and take the opportunity to strengthen the regulator's focus on innovation and foresight.
    - **Fully implement** the announced restructuring and provide staff with a clear deadline for its completion
- **Introduce** the Innovation and Special Projects Office and include foresight functions in its terms of reference, to consolidate understanding on changes taking place in the sector. This office could report directly to the board and support its strategic function of looking at future challenges and opportunities in the industry. This office could bring in expertise from outside the regulator (e.g. academia, energy sector more broadly) for limited periods (e.g. 6 months) to work at ERSE on specific technical areas.
- **Establish** "communities of practice" bringing together staff from across the organisation and from other public authorities and regulators interested in particular topics (Box 9). For example, there could be a community of practice on distributed energy or on the implications of electric mobility.
- **Respond** to the evolving needs of the organisation as it grows.
    - **Design and codify** formal internal processes, for example around data collection and management, use of regulatory management tools etc.

### Box 9. Creating "communities of practice"

Regulators have established communities of practice bringing together staff interested in particular topics as a way to share knowledge and stay abreast of latest developments.

**Professional Networks at Sweden's Post and Telecom Authority (PTS)**

At the Swedish Post and Telecom Authority (PTS), several internal professional networks provide the opportunity for staff members from different departments and units to come together and discuss topics of mutual interest. The structure and set-up of the networks differ depending on the theme and purpose and may shift over time. Topics include workshop facilitation, competitive intelligence or simply providing a forum for all the lawyers in the authority to meet and discuss.

One of the more long-standing and established networks is themed around supervision. PTS is organised so that supervision of market actors takes place in different departments and based on different legislation and regulations. The Supervision fora is a chance for all staff members actively working on supervision to exchange views and ideas but also a way for PTS to try to ensure coherence in its processes across departments. Although the supervision is based to some extent on different legal frameworks, and there may be justified reasons for different approaches, the aim is to have coherent processes when possible.

The fora meets twice a year and in-between there are possibilities for exchange of information on ongoing cases or other interesting topics. Often there are external speakers invited as well, providing perspectives on supervision from other regulators or, for example, the Parliamentary Ombudsmen, that responsible for ensuring that public authorities and their staff comply with the laws and other statues governing their actions.

The fora is administrated by a group of staff members working on supervision in different departments.

Source: Information provided by PTS, 2020.

**Communities of Practice at the Australian Competition and Consumer Commission (ACCC) and the Australian Energy Regulator (AER)**

The ACCC/AER has several internal "communities of practice". For example, there is a community of practice on distributed energy. The regulator also has internal "networks" which bring together like-minded people using specific tools or approaches. For example, there is a "Quantitative Analysis Network" that meets regularly to discuss and learn about tools and techniques for quantitative analysis (such as R, excel, python). An "Economics Network" meets to share issues and developments in economics.

Source: Information provided by ACCC/AER, 2020.

## *Regulatory quality tools*

***Ex ante* assessments of regulations are not used systematically and there is no standard methodology for carrying out assessments, which could generate inconsistencies in approach.** No formal *ex ante* assessment is mandatory for ERSE activities, except in some areas where they are required under European regulation.[8] Although ERSE does not undertake systematic *ex ante* assessment of costs and benefits, every ERSE decision must be subject to formal hearings and must be accompanied by a justification document. The justification document may include scenario analysis, impact evaluation, explanation of the regulation's intention, its legal framework, etc. There is no explicit proportionality requirement for ERSE to tailor the level of the assessment to the potential impacts of a new regulation.

**Nevertheless, the level of detail used in the *ex ante* analysis depends on the type of decision and its general impacts**. For decisions on tariffs and regulated companies' revenues, the economic analysis is detailed and data on costs and benefits is usually included. Currently, each head of division is responsible for determining whether a cost-benefit analysis is needed and for coordinating the analysis. Generally, the benefits assessed in the CBAs amount to the costs avoided for the regulated sectors. The methodology does not tend to assess other types of costs and benefits, such as societal, environmental etc. or include equality and diversity assessments. A new unit (GGI) is currently being established in the context of ERSE's restructuration that will review and develop internal processes and quality control procedures, including for CBAs.

ERSE undertakes *ex post* reviews within the tariff-setting process and at the end of a regulatory period (every 3 or 4 years, depending on the sector). However, these do not follow a standard methodology across all sectors regulated, and do not encompass sufficient regard as to the quality of the regulatory setting process or of the regulatory tools employed by the regulator.

*Recommendations*

- **Develop** a standardised approach for and increase the use of regulatory impact assessments on new regulatory policies, proportional to the significance of the regulation, to boost the quality of regulation.
- **Include** *ex ante* assessments in all justification documents prepared for stakeholder consultations. When doing so, care should be taken to use clear and simple language to facilitate access to a broad audience.
- **Put in place** corporate processes and detailed guidance material to ensure a consistent approach to regulatory impact assessments. Certain regulations may not require a full-fledged, quantitative cost-benefit analysis. There may be synergies with work on-going at the central government level in the Technical Unit for Legislative Impact Assessment (UTAIL). UTAIL is developing an impact assessment methodology, giving technical support and providing training to ministries and other bodies from the public administration.
- **Identify** all relevant direct and important indirect costs as well as benefits. Consider assessing a wider range of costs and benefits, such as societal, environmental as well as costs avoided for regulated sector. Similarly, equality and diversity assessments (e.g. assessments on the most financially vulnerable consumers) would help ensure that regulations do not disproportionately affect disadvantaged groups.
- **Develop** a standardised and systematic approach for *ex post* assessments of ERSE regulations, together with a communications strategy which allows the market and consumers to understand the impact and effectiveness of ERSE's economic regulations.

### *Audit, inspections and enforcement*

**The audit process is relatively more transparent than inspections, but neither process uses a risk-based approach.** ERSE carried out 13 audits and 8 inspections between 2015 and 2019. Portuguese legislation does not require audits and inspections to be risk-based. The Framework Law of Independent Administrative Entities establishes that regulators shall carry out inspections and audits on an *ad hoc* basis, in execution of previously approved plans and/or whenever there are circumstances that indicate disturbances in the respective sector of activity (for example, complaints). ERSE has two categories of audits: one-off specialised audits triggered by the identification of potential non-compliance, and regular audits, generally on an annual basis. In the case of entities that are subject to the Tariff Regulation, ERSE approves an auditing and oversight plan containing the issues subject to periodic auditing. The plan does not include a calendar of audits, but ERSE notifies regulated companies by letter well in advance that an audit is due to take place. Specialised audit firms selected by ERSE carry out the audits whereas ERSE carries out inspections itself. In the past, ERSE has had annual inspection plans but more recently has carried out inspections on a needs-based approach, based on data analysis and monitoring of the regulated companies. The regulator can also decide to take action because of consumer complaints. The ERSE website publishes reports on the outcomes of some but not all audits; it does not publish data or information on the outcomes of inspections (ERSE, 2020[2]).

**Sanctioning procedures are transparent but the diverse legal frameworks that underpin ERSE's sanctioning powers lead to different enforcement outcomes. In some sectors sanctions may not be an adequate deterrent.** Stakeholders commend ERSE for its transparent sanctioning procedures. All procedures are public and searchable on request. ERSE can impose a wide range of sanctions, including warnings, fines and accessory sanctions.[9] Under the Energy Sector Sanctions Framework[10] the gradation of available sanctions is considered adequate to allow credible deterrence through the escalation of sanctions. The maximum fine is 10% of total turnover depending on the seriousness of the administrative offence for legal persons and 30% of total annual remuneration for natural persons, and can be doubled for repeat offenders. The Energy Sector Sanctions Framework applies to the electricity and natural gas sectors but does not cover fuels, electric mobility and the EU's REMIT Regulation. Different legislation, in particular the special penalty regimes, confers sanctioning powers to ERSE in the other sectors. Fines are limited to a maximum of EUR 15 000 under the complaints book rules and EUR 44 891.81 under unfair trading practices. Several cases of repeat offenders indicate that the sanctions under these special penalty regimes are not a credible deterrent.

*Recommendations:*

- **Ensure** inspections and enforcement are risk-based and proportionate. Decisions on what to inspect and how should be grounded in data and evidence, and results should be evaluated regularly (Box 10).
- **Advocate** for change to sanctioning regimes to ensure sanctions are credible deterrent.

### Box 10. Identification of priorities through risk tables at the UK's Health and Safety Executive

A number of tools can be implemented as part of developing a risk-based approach in relation to the inspection plan. For instance, the build-up of the risk table is a useful instrument which aids to the identification of priorities.

For instance, the approach in the table below was developed by the Health and Safety Executive England in order to determine the risk gap. This table matches the consequence and likelihood of the actual risk with the consequence and likelihood of the benchmark risk. In this manner, the regulator knows where to focus its efforts as part of their inspection activities. This leads to more targeted enforcement activity designed to counter the actual higher risk to consumers, as well as allows the regulator to identify areas of activity where a market actor might need additional guidance or education from the regulator.

Furthermore, an analysis of the areas flagged consistently as high risk over a longer period, enables a regulator to identify and investigate whether there are systematic deficiencies with the substance of the regulation, or with the interpretation of regulation by the market actors.

**Figure 3. Risk matrix at the HSE UK**

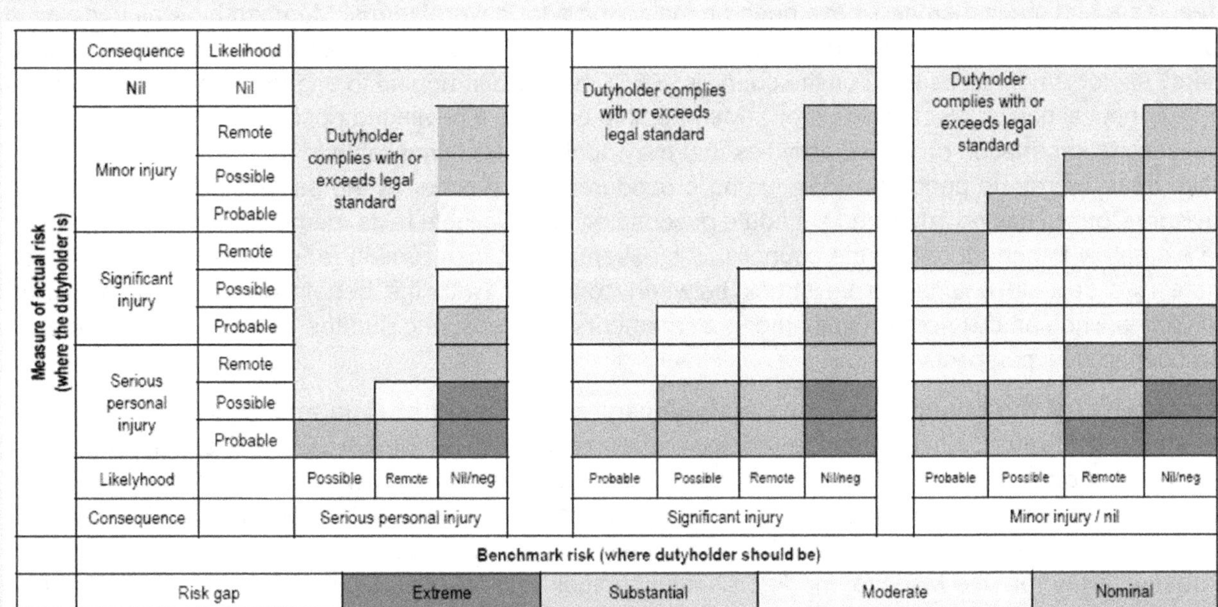


Note: This figure is an edited version, for brevity and clarity.

Source: Health and Safety Executive, Enforcement Management Model, HSE, http://www.hse.gov.uk/enforce/emm.pdf (accessed 21 September 2020).

### *Engagement and transparency of engagement process*

**ERSE counts on several mechanisms for consultation that enable differentiated degrees of stakeholder engagement depending on the nature of the regulation**. All decisions on codes and regulations must be preceded by a public consultation or a stakeholder consultation in the case of tariff decisions. ERSE also organises public hearings in the majority of regulatory reviews to promote more dynamic and interactive discussions. For particularly complex or sensitive issues, ERSE may conduct pre-consultations before the presentation of the regulation proposal in order to identify stakeholders' main concerns. ERSE also has three independent advisory bodies – the Advisory Council, the Tariff Council and the Fuels Council – that provide opinions on all decisions.

**The three consultative councils are constructive, transparent structures for engagement with major stakeholders that bring value to ERSE's decision-making and to Portugal's energy sector more broadly.** ERSE consults on its various decisions with its key stakeholders through three independent advisory bodies that deliver non-binding opinions: the Advisory Council, the Tariff Council and, since 2019, the Fuels Council. All opinions of the councils are approved by majority vote, although if members do not agree with all or parts of the opinion of the council they can state this in the submission to ERSE. The opinions of the councils are made public and published on the ERSE website (ERSE, 2020[3]). If the opinions of the councils do not lead to a change in ERSE's proposed decision, the regulator must justify why it is not making the suggested changes. The councils are an important space within the energy sector for stakeholders to gather and understand each other's positions, in addition to the value that they bring to ERSE in terms of ensuring that its decision-making is more accountable and robust.

**The councils include a wide variety of perspectives and membership bestows a privileged position to members.** The councils are composed of members defined under the law including industry, consumer representatives, representatives from other regulatory entities or public bodies and, in the case of the

Advisory Council, government representatives from both national and regional levels. Industry and consumer representatives must be represented in equal numbers. Members serve a renewable term of three years and many members have been on the councils for several terms. Membership was updated in legislation two years ago. Some segments of the energy sector are less represented (e.g. the renewable energy sector is not represented on the councils; ERSE has also struggled to engage with relevant players for its consultations on electric mobility[11]). Membership bestows a privileged position to members in terms of access to information on ERSE activities that may not be publicly available to all stakeholders at large. While there are some periodic and recurring procedures which occur at the same time every year, the Advisory Council has no advanced schedule of consultations available to its members or the public. Given the extremely important role of the councils, it is essential that they remain representative of the sector. There is a delicate balance to be struck between continuity (with the benefit of experienced, skilled presidents who can build consensus among all members) and ensuring that the councils remain dynamic and open to new perspectives.

**Membership of the councils requires a significant commitment of time and resources given the growing workload.** Councils provide opinions when requested by the ERSE president. Each council decides how often to meet in order to address these requests, but in general the work entails several meetings a month and sometimes several a week at the ERSE headquarters in Lisbon. Members are expected to travel to all meetings, including members based outside the Lisbon area such as representatives from the Madeira and Azores archipelagos (a three-hour flight in the case of the Azores). The organisations that members represent are not remunerated for their participation. However, in order to facilitate the participation of household consumer representatives, ERSE allocates a per diem to these members. Over time, the range of issues that councils discuss has expanded. ERSE sometimes asks councils to provide opinions on the same issue several times. Members of the councils may also submit opinions twice: once via the consensus opinion of their council and again from their organisation alone via the standard public consultation process.

**Consultation through these formal channels is transparent. Information on interactions with stakeholders outside these processes is less accessible to the public.** ERSE can hold meetings with stakeholders to hear from specific perspectives outside the broader public consultation process. ERSE does not publish a list of these meetings or their minutes. Separately, ERSE may have meetings with formal "support groups" composed of stakeholders, for which the documentation and minutes are kept for legal and administrative purposes. This information is not published, but can be accessed upon request (e.g. freedom of information provisions and right of recourse of administrative procedures).

**ERSE combines rigorous consultation processes with quicker processes in urgent and extraordinary cases, allowing for nimble decision-making when required.** As of June 2020, ERSE concluded a total of 87 public consultations sine its creation. On average, consultations have lasted 144 days (5 months); in two cases, the process took two years to complete. The regulator's statutes allow ERSE to hold short 8-day consultations in "urgent and "extraordinary" cases, reflected in the regulator's agility during the COVID-19 crisis. Following an urgent public consultation in April 2020, ERSE adopted a regulation that extends the current regulatory period for the electricity sector by one year, to the end of 2021. ERSE reasoned that the degree of unpredictability created by the pandemic prevents a consistent definition of new regulatory goals and methodologies to take effect in a new regulatory period.

*Recommendations:*

- **Continue** with the highly positive practice of consultative councils and preserve their value through proportionate use.
    - **Share** the good practice of consultative councils with regulators in Portugal and internationally.

  - **Carefully consider** which decisions or issues should go to councils, for example by establishing a document that sets out expectations for each council and sets targets on the number of meeting days per year.
  - **Publish** an advance schedule of consultations for visibility and predictability for Council members but also to the wider public, in the interest of transparency.
  - **Modernise** working methods, for example, by making participation in meetings more flexible for members based outside of Lisbon (e.g. use of video-conferencing). Lessons learnt from teleworking and restrictions on movement during the COVID-19 pandemic can support this objective.
  - **Work** with the executive to regularly review and analyse council membership to ensure representativeness as the market evolves. This would keep the council membership relevant to the current challenges facing the sector and allow new players to participate as they join the sector.
- **Increase** access to information for all stakeholders, not only those on councils. The revamped ERSE website could be a key tool to make available information such as the list of forthcoming consultations, all public consultation materials, board decisions, and information on inspections, audits, enforcement and appeals.
- **Improve** transparency around interactions with stakeholders outside of the formal public consultations processes. For example, ERSE Board members could publish their calendars online and a registry of meetings with stakeholders could be kept by the regulator. If appropriate, the main outcomes or decisions or these meetings could also be released.
- **Continue** the proportionate use of consultations, including the use of 'fast track' processes in case of emergency. In the interest of predictability, decisions made in "urgent" and "extraordinary" cases must be based on transparent criteria and when possible and relevant, subject to post implementation reviews. For example, such an assessment of ERSE's response to the COVID-19 crisis would constitute good candidates for such review.

## Output and outcome

### *Data collection, management and analysis*

**Reporting requirements for regulated entities are predictable and detailed.** ERSE regulations require regulated entities to submit a large amount of data at differing frequencies depending on the type of information. Data reporting requirements are generally defined for the regulatory period (three years for the electricity sector and four years for the natural gas sector), which provides some stability and predictability for regulated entities. ERSE has the right nevertheless to request additional information whenever it deems it necessary. There is no formal or periodic review of reporting requirements, however, ERSE often reviews reporting obligations in terms of their usefulness in order to adapt to changes in the market or regulation. If the need does arise to adjust the reporting requirements, a formal process is launched and new rules are published.

**Simple tools are in place to avoid companies receiving multiple data requests from different divisions, but there is no central portal for actors to submit data to ERSE or co-ordination with other public bodies**. Each ERSE division requests data from entities pertaining to their respective areas of work. To co-ordinate the different data requests, divisions have access to a shared email account from which the data requests are sent to avoid companies receiving messages from several different contact points within ERSE. Divisions also rely on informal communications between staff to stay informed about what data is being requested from which companies. This system appears to be working for the moment as companies report that it is rare to receive repeat requests for information. However, companies often need to report the same data to DGEG, who has responsibility for compiling Portugal's energy statistics, and ENSE, which has supervisory responsibilities across the whole energy sector. There is no common database within ERSE or between ERSE and other bodies for the whole energy sector, although ERSE uses the "Balcão Unico" system, a joint platform shared by ERSE, ENSE, LNEG and DGEG, hosted by ENSE, for supervising and monitoring the petroleum products and biofuels sectors. ENSE has proposed to extend this joint platform to the electricity and natural gas sectors.

**ERSE has recognised the need for sophisticated data management and analysis capabilities to realise the opportunities from 'big data'.** Given the volume of data required by the regulatory process and supervision activities, ERSE has been implementing a strategy for using and structuring data using business intelligence tools and IT systems. In autumn 2019, ERSE launched an internal working group to review and map the various data and communication tools used by the divisions, with a view to developing a strategy for their efficiency, interoperability and modernisation. ERSE is investing in IT systems that will enable the establishment of more complete databases that can support new uses and data processing. In addition, several projects are underway to make various data collection obligations "smarter" and more automated.

### *Monitoring and reporting on the performance of the sector and the regulator*

**ERSE monitors the performance of regulated entities, the direct outcomes of its regulatory decisions and wider outcomes, in particular the performance of the wholesale and retail markets and consumer welfare.** ERSE makes public much of the information it receives from regulated entities at an aggregated level in reports and in the documents that it prepares for public or stakeholder consultation. However, much of the data that ERSE handles is commercially sensitive or confidential and therefore not published. ERSE reports on the performance of the sector include reporting on service quality, economic and financial performance (e.g. investment monitoring), competition, security of supply and consumer protection. ERSE carries out systematic *ex post* analysis of the impact of regulatory period for both electricity and gas markets to inform regulatory decision making for the next period. These reports include analysis of the performance of different sectors of the market as well as individual market actors. The reports are published on the ERSE website.

**The regulator does not report against a comprehensive set of performance indicators but is currently working on addressing this gap.** The strategic plan 2019-2022 was finalised in 2019 but the associated performance indicators have still to be defined; the work is ongoing. Each division is devising indicators for its activities that they will submit to the Board for approval in 2020. This bottom up approach may run the risk that the indicators do not capture overall corporate performance or performance on cross-cutting goals as defined by the strategic plan, but rather focus on the activities and deliverables of individual teams. The delay in defining indicators also deprives ERSE of a tool to track whether it is meeting the goals it set out in its strategy. At the time of the review, no information was available to assess whether the performance indicators would capture the quality of processes, the outcomes of activities and the overall sector performance.

**ERSE fulfils its legislative reporting requirements but could do more to demonstrate its impact and value to key external stakeholders.** Legislation requires ERSE to publish a report on its activities on a regular basis.[12] The Board prepares an annual report and accounts that is approved by the government and the parliament and published on the ERSE website. ERSE is not invited to present the report to parliament for discussion. The annual report is a comprehensive and in parts technical report (~165 pages) of ERSE's activities that includes the regulations and codes emitted by ERSE and all the formal opinions published by ERSE in the course of the year. The report may not be accessible to all parliamentarians and other stakeholders due to the highly technical presentation of some of the information. Outside of the annual reporting process, the ERSE president occasionally presents to the parliament upon its invitation, during which members may ask them about the regulator's performance. In addition, ERSE reports annually to the European Commission and the Agency for the Cooperation of Energy Regulators (ACER) on its activities and the developments in the Portuguese electricity and natural gas markets.

*Recommendations:*

- **Reduce** regulatory burden for the sector by streamlining data collection and management within ERSE and collaborating on a "one-stop shop" across the energy sector.
    - **Establish** a common database within ERSE and a unified system for contacting regulated entities with data requests. As data reporting requirements evolve and the collection of 'big data' gathers pace, the simple system for co-ordination between divisions in ERSE currently in place may not be sufficient to avoid companies receiving duplicated requests for data.
    - **Extend** the successful experience of the "*Balcão Unico*" system for the fuels sector to create a "one-stop shop" for all energy sectors between ERSE, DGEG, ENSE and any other relevant bodies for data collection, and ideally for all administrative processes. One-stop shops are a critical component of regulatory delivery and can help maximise the potential gains of regulatory reduction. The OECD *Best Practice Principles on One-Stop Shops for Citizens and Business* (OECD, 2020[3]) offers general guidance on one-stop shops under two overarching principles: that they should form part of broader administrative simplification strategies and be user-centred and based on life events. In this way, they can help bring public entities closer to citizens and business in the least burdensome way possible.
- **Monitor** ERSE's own performance using the strategic framework to define performance indicators for the organisation.
    - **Define** the performance indicators for the current strategic plan as a matter of urgency. Indicators should capture the quality of processes (e.g. the time taken to reach a decision, whether responses are given to comments received during stakeholder consultations in a timely manner etc...), the outcomes of activities, and the overall sector performance and be accompanied by time-bound, measurable targets.
    - **Incorporate** performance measures into planning systems; investigate and act when practice is diverging significantly from established targets.
    - **Continue** the good practice of carrying out a periodic qualitative survey of stakeholders to obtain information on awareness about ERSE.
- **Use** reporting as an opportunity to showcase the value of independent economic regulation to key external stakeholders. ERSE could demonstrate its value by showing the impact of its activities to a wide range of stakeholders through clear, results-based communications.
    - **Report** against the delivery of the strategic framework either through the Annual Report and Accounts (e.g. include a section on strategic reporting) and/or publish an overall assessment on the delivery of strategy at the end of the four-year period.
    - **Apply** ERSE's proven skills of communicating with consumers to the task of reporting on its own performance. ERSE has considerable experience in using plain language suited to a non-technical audience in its communications with consumers. A similar approach could be taken to its communications around its own performance.
    - **Consider preparing** an annual publication intended for interested parties in the sector as a whole, such as a "State of the Energy Market" publication (Box 11). The objective of such a publication would be to a) solidify ERSE's reputation as a key source of information in the sector; b) communicate how ERSE is working in the different components of the sector for the long-term interests of consumers; c) communicate how the regulatory framework operates to clarify what does and does not fall within the responsibility of ERSE (thereby helping stakeholders to know the limits to what ERSE can achieve); and (d) to build a broader

community of interested members of the sector and members of the public which are invested in the performance of ERSE.

- **More regular engagement with parliament** could increase accountability as well as improve understanding among legislators on the role and value of independent economic regulation for the energy sector.

### Box 11. Australian Energy Regulator's "State of the Energy Market" publication

The Australian Energy Regulator's flagship publication is the annual "State of the Energy Market" report. This publication provides statistics, analysis and insights on each of the major components of the energy sector and each of the major policy developments. In a sector which is transforming rapidly, and in which it is hard to keep up with all the developments, the State of the Energy Market report has become essential reading for the sector and an important source of information for journalists and stakeholders.

The release of the State of the Energy Market report is accompanied by a press release and a round of engagement with the media by the Chair of the AER, including interviews with print, television and radio. This is an opportunity for the AER to gain some exposure in the mainstream media and establish itself as a trusted and authoritative source of information. It is also an opportunity for the AER to highlight key trends in the industry, both to highlight what is working well (to forestall pressure for further regulatory intervention) and to highlight emerging problems (to identify future regulatory issues).

The most recent State of the Energy Market (released on 1 July 2020) also highlights some of the key regulatory and policy work of the AER, including its work facilitating the integration of renewable generation, its decisions on new innovative network tariffs, and its work in developing the *EnergyMadeEasy* website, which is designed to facilitate comparison-shopping of retailers by consumers. In addition, the report highlights the actions taken by the AER in response to the COVID crisis, including its Statement of Expectations for the behaviour of electricity retailers during the crisis (including the expectation that they will not disconnect customers in financial distress).

In short, the State of the Energy Market, as an accessible yet informative publication, has allowed the AER to gain greater profile and exposure and to increase the confidence of policy makers and the broader community in its work. As the Chair of the AER (Clare Savage) says in the accompanying press release: "Our State of the Energy Market Report is a valuable resource that helps us all better understand the drivers of change as we transition into a new model while managing the impact of COVID-19."

Sources: Information provided by AER, 2020. AER, State of the Energy Market, 2020. https://www.aer.gov.au/publications/state-of-the-energy-market-reports/state-of-the-energy-market-2020 (accessed March 2021). AER's State of the Energy Market 2020 outlines rapid evolution of energy sector, AER, https://www.aer.gov.au/news-release/aer%E2%80%99s-state-of-the-energy-market-2020-outlines-rapid-evolution-of-energy-sector (accessed March 2021).

## Notes

[1] Three peer reviewers participated in the mission: Darryl Biggar, Special Economic Adviser, Australian Competition and Consumer Commission (ACCC), Australia; Laura Brien, Director of Water and

Compliance, Commission for Regulation of Utilities (CRU), Ireland; and Emma Närvä, Deputy Director for International Affairs and Senior Policy Adviser, Swedish Post and Telecom Authority (PTS), Sweden.

[2] Financing is divided between Portugal's economic regulators for telecommunications (ANACOM), water and waste services (ERSAR) and ERSE, as the arbitration centres handle complaints from all three utility sectors, classified as essential services.

[3] See Articles 10, 16, 59 (1 and 3) of ERSE Statutes and Article 59: Cooperation with the Government and Assembleia da República.

[4] The independence indicator maps the degree to which a regulator operates independently and with no undue influence from both the political power and the regulated sectors. Questions are organised into three subsections: relationship with the executive, staff and budget. It seeks to measure aspects of *de facto* independence through a variety of dimensions beyond only *de jure* independence.

[5] Redes Energéticas Nacionais (REN) is the current concession holder of both the national electricity transmission grid and the national natural gas transportation grid.

[6] The government took three former ERSE Board members to court following their refusal to pass the surplus to the national treasury. In 2017, the former board members were convicted, fined EUR 2 550 each and ERSE was forced to transfer the surplus plus interest to the national treasury.

[7] By contrast, salaries of the Board members are capped in law.

[8] ERSE has recently been mandated by the government and by the parliament to perform CBA studies on planned pipeline projects in the context of the National Petroleum System. These CBAs are to inform the government's/parliament's decision making rather than a regulatory management tool for ERSE's own regulatory decision making.

[9] Prohibition of the exercise of any activity within the scope of the regulated sectors, banning of the exercise of an administrative or management position in entities intervening in the regulated sectors and publication in a national expansion newspaper or on ERSE's website.

[10] See The Energy Sector Sanctions Framework, approved by Law No. 9/2013, of 28 January.

[11] There is no consultative council for the electric mobility sector which posed challenges for ERSE in terms of identifying relevant stakeholders to consult when it launched a public consultation pertaining to this sector. To make up for this gap, the Infrastructure and Networks Division within ERSE has established informal stakeholder groups with which to interact on this subject.

[12] Article 7 of ERSE statutes; http://www.erse.pt/pt/aerse/instrumentosdegestao/relatoriosecontas/Paginas/default.aspx.

## References

ERSE (2020), *Enforcement*, https://www.erse.pt/en/activities/enforcement/ (accessed on 16 December 2020). [2]

OECD (2020), *One-Stop Shops for Citizens and Business*, OECD Best Practice Principles for Regulatory Policy, OECD Publishing, Paris, https://dx.doi.org/10.1787/b0b0924e-en. [3]

OECD (2014), *Regulatory Enforcement and Inspections*, OECD Best Practice Principles for Regulatory Policy, OECD Publishing, Paris, https://dx.doi.org/10.1787/9789264208117-en. [1]

# 1 Regulatory and sector context

This chapter provides an overview of Portugal's public institutions and describes the main features of the energy sector as well as the legislative framework that determines the functions of Portugal's *Entidade Reguladora dos Serviços Energéticos* (ERSE).

## Institutional framework

Portugal is a parliamentary republic with a unicameral parliament, an executive branch headed by a prime minister and a directly elected president (Figure 1.1). The national legislative body is the National Assembly (Parliament), with members elected by universal suffrage. The Assembly has responsibilities over political, legislative and fiscal matters.

The two autonomous regions of the Azores and Madeira are archipelagos located in the Atlantic Ocean with their own political and administrative statutes and their own institutions of self-government (Eurydice, 2019[1]).

### Figure 1.1. Portugal's public institutions

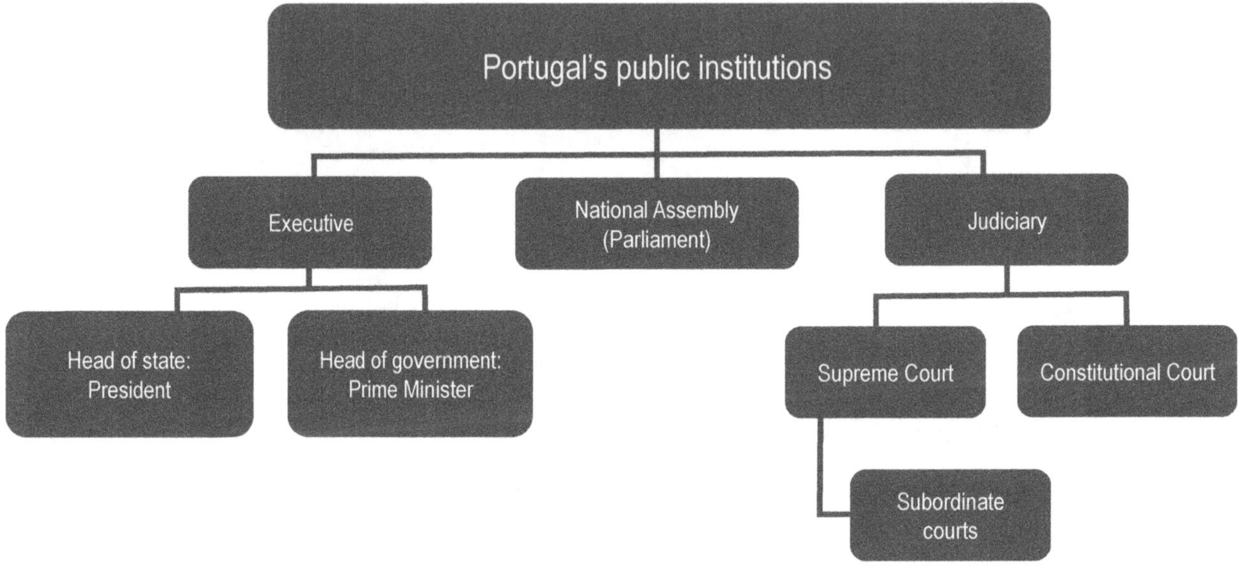


## Portugal's energy sector

### *Energy supply and demand*

In 2018, fossil fuels accounted for 75% of Portugal's total primary energy supply (TPES) (Figure 1.2). Oil was the largest energy source, accounting for 40% of TPES. Demand for oil originates mainly from the transport and industry sectors as well as building heating. Natural gas was the second-largest energy source, accounting for 23% of TPES and was used mainly for electricity generation, industrial processes and a small share for building heating. Bioenergy and waste covered 14% of TPES and supported electricity generation and building heating. Coal accounted for 12% of TPES and was used mainly for electricity generation. Small shares of TPES came from hydro (5%), wind (5%), covering electricity generation, and from geothermal (1%) and solar (1%), covering electricity generation and building heating. All fossil fuels are imported and domestic energy production comes primarily from renewables, mainly bioenergy, hydropower and wind.

Coal is mainly used for the production of electricity; its falling contribution to TPES is linked with an increase in greener sources of electricity, such as wind and solar power, which has seen a significant increase of 34% between 2010 and 2018.

## Figure 1.2. Total primary energy supply by source, 2000-18

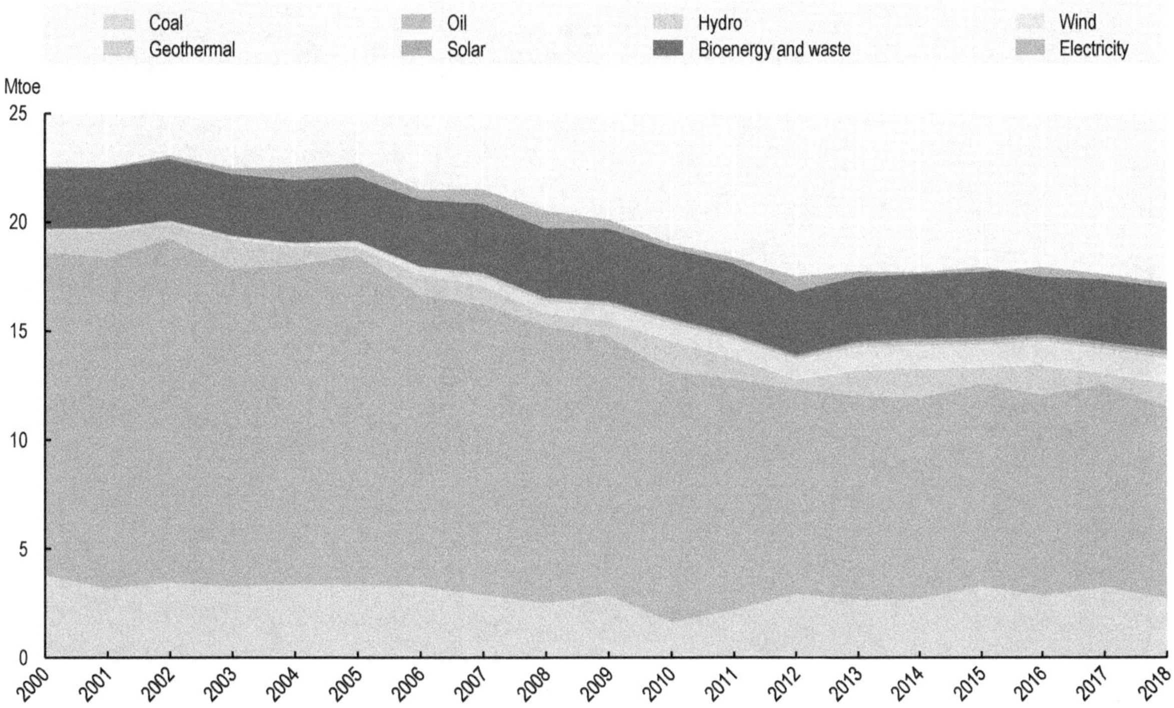

Source: IEA (2020), World Energy Balances 2020, www.iea.org/statistics/.

Total electricity generation in Portugal was 58.4 TWh in 2018. From 2000 to 2018 electricity generation increased by around 35%. However, there were notable annual variations in total generation because of changing levels of economic activity and electricity trade (Figure 1.3). Since 2016, the growth in electricity generation (especially from wind) has turned Portugal from a net importer to a net exporter of electricity. In 2018, natural gas accounted for 27% of total electricity generation followed by wind (22%), hydro (21%), coal (21%), bioenergy and waste (6%), oil (2%) and solar (2%).

Since 2000, hydropower has accounted for 10% to 34% of total generation, with the contribution varying significantly based on hydrological conditions. Bioenergy and waste have accounted for a notable and slowly growing share of generation for several decades. The share of generation from wind power increased significantly from 12% of generation in 2000 to 22% in 2018, to become the second largest source of electricity. Generation from solar photovoltaics (PV), while still small, has been rapidly increasing. Because of the large variation in hydro generation, the overall share of electricity generation from renewables varies notably from year to year. The renewable share peaked at 62% of generation in 2014 and dropped to 40% in 2017. However, the overall trend has been a steady increase in the share of renewable generation, driven by investments in wind and hydropower.

The share of generation from oil has declined substantially from 9% in 2008 to just 2% in 2018. Generation from coal and natural gas continue to play a major role in Portugal with the share from each fuel affected by the comparative cost of electricity from coal versus natural gas and by the level of hydro generation. Generation from natural gas has been more volatile, ranging from 13% to 33% of generation from 2008 to 2018. Generation from coal has been relatively stable, generally around 20% to 25% of generation from 2008 to 2018, but with a notable drop to 13% in 2010 because of a large increase in hydro generation and steady natural gas generation. However, the share of coal generation is expected to drop as the government has committed to closing coal-fired power plants before 2030, and introduced a tax on coal based electricity generation in 2018 that will be progressively increased through 2023 (IEEFA, 2020[2]).

Figure 1.3. Electricity generation in Portugal by source, 2000-18

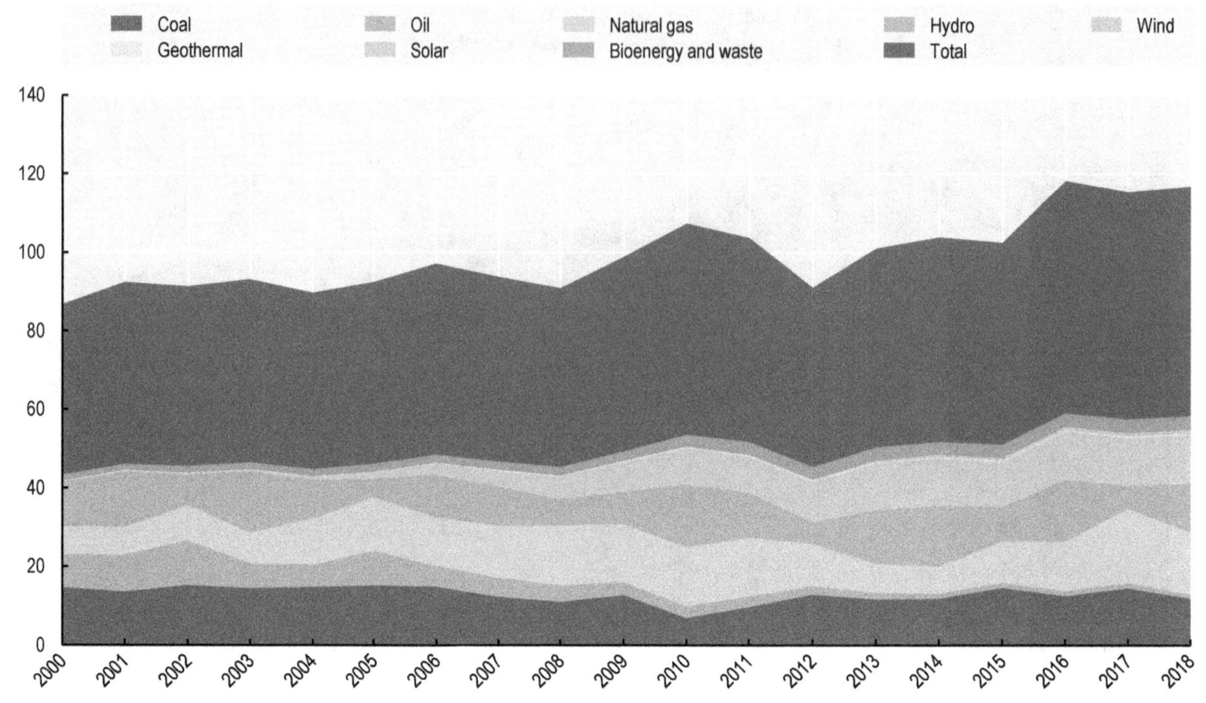

Source: IEA (2020), World Energy Balances 2020, www.iea.org/statistics.

## *Energy policy*

Portugal has taken action to reduce the environmental impact of the energy sector in recent years, by establishing several policies that aim to increase the use of renewable energy, improve energy efficiency, decrease energy import dependency and improve the economic sustainability of the energy system (OECD, 2020[3]).

In 2016, the Portuguese government committed to an emissions-neutral economy by the end of 2050, as a contribution to the Paris Agreement and in line with ongoing international efforts. It submitted its 2050 Carbon Neutrality Roadmap to the United Nations in September 2019 (Portugal Gov, 2020[4]) and its National Energy Climate Plan (NECP) 2030 to the European Commission in December 2019 (Portugal Energia, 2020[5]). The NECP 2030 is the main document that defines energy and climate policy for the 2021-2030 decade, in support of the Carbon Neutrality Roadmap.

In some instances, Portugal's energy and climate policy goes beyond EU requirements. In line with Directive 2012/27 EU (Energy Efficiency Directive) (Union, 2012[6]), Portugal needed to reduce primary energy consumption by 20% by 2020 compared to 2007 (EC, n.d.[7]). A more ambitious 2020 target of a 25% reduction was subsequently adopted by Portugal (EC, 2017[8]), showing its commitment to transition to a greener economy.

One of the main objectives of the national energy policy is to reduce energy import dependency. Portugal has a high energy import dependency due to the lack of domestic production of fossil fuels, which cover most of the country's energy demand. In 2018, Portugal's import dependency was 85%, one of the highest levels among OECD countries (IEA, 2020[9]). However, the increasing level of domestic energy production coming from renewable energy is helping to reduce import dependency. In 2014, strong hydropower generation and the steady increase in wind generation reduced energy import dependency to a record low of 77%. From 2000 to 2008 energy import dependency averaged 89%. Thanks to renewable energy average import dependency from 2009 to 2018 was down to 83%.

### Market structure

Portugal's markets for electricity and gas are liberalised and open for competition. However, previously state-owned energy companies continue to have large market shares. The privatisation and legal unbundling of the state-owned Electricidade de Portugal (now EDP S.A.) started in 1997. The EDP S.A. group has a large presence in Portugal through its subsidiaries, both in the electricity and gas markets. REN was a state-owned company that took ownership of the transmission network of the electricity market at the unbundling stage in 1997 and is currently privately owned.

#### *Electricity market and key institutions (mainland Portugal)*

**Generation and wholesale market**: EDP is the largest generator in the electricity wholesale market in Portugal and held a market share of 43% in 2018, in comparison to 52% in 2009 (Eurostat, 2020[10]). EDP also acts as an aggregating market participant for several hundred individual renewable energy generators with guaranteed tariff scheme under the national law, as the supplier of last resort through a subsidiary company with a separate brand (SU Eletricidade) that is regulated by ERSE. Market-based generation is not regulated by ERSE. The Iberian Electricity Market (MIBEL) is the integrated electricity market between Portugal and Spain. MIBEL has a common spot market operator (OMIE) and a forward market operator (OMIP).

**Transmission**: REN (*Rede Elétrica Nacional*), is the operator (TSO) of the National Electricity Transmission Network. It was certified by ERSE in 2015 as the TSO under a full ownership unbundling regime. As the TSO, REN is "responsible for the planning, implementation and operation of the national transmission grid, the related infrastructure, as well as all of the relevant interconnections and other facilities necessary to operate the national transmission grid" (IEA, 2016[11]).

**Distribution**: E-Redes (previously EDP Distribuição[1], an EDP S.A. subsidiary) is the largest Portuguese distribution network operator (DSO) with more than 5 million customers. In addition, there are 10 more small distribution operators in the mainland that serve around 30 000 customers. The distribution activity in mainland Portugal is developed according to a public service concession regime at two levels: i) a single concession of the national distribution network at medium voltage (MV) and high voltage (HV) assigned by the state; and ii) the municipal low voltage (LV) concessions granted by the country's 278 municipalities. The LV concessions have a term of 20 years ending at different times between 2016 and 2026. The majority will cease between 2021 and 2022. Their attribution must result from a public tender.

**Retail markets:** Portugal was expected to complete the liberalisation process in the retail markets for electricity and natural gas by the end of 2015, but the end of regulated tariffs has been extended[2] to new deadlines.[3]

The liberalised market accounted for about 94% of total consumption in mainland Portugal in August 2019. Virtually all consumption of large consumers is on the liberalised market. For domestic consumers, liberalised market consumption is about 86% of the total segment. The liberalised market has consolidated its position, mainly due to the process of phasing out end-user regulated tariffs that, in January 2013, started to cover all the clients including household customers.

At the end of 2018 there were 29 free market agents, of which 26 served residential customers and small companies. Despite the growth of the liberalised market, overall market concentration remained high in 2018. The incumbent (EDP Group) retains a large market share at over 40% of supply in 2019 (Figure 1.4). EDP is also the supplier of last resort for electricity (regulated prices).

Since 2018, a new legislative provision allows electricity customers in the liberalised market to opt for the same end-user tariffs as the regulated transitional ones, to be offered by suppliers in the liberalised market. If their supplier does not participate in this new regime, customers can opt to be supplied by the supplier of last resort. However, this new regime did not have substantive effects in terms of the return of consumers to the supplier of last resort.

**Figure 1.4. Supply structure in the liberalised market for electricity**

By market agent, 2015-19

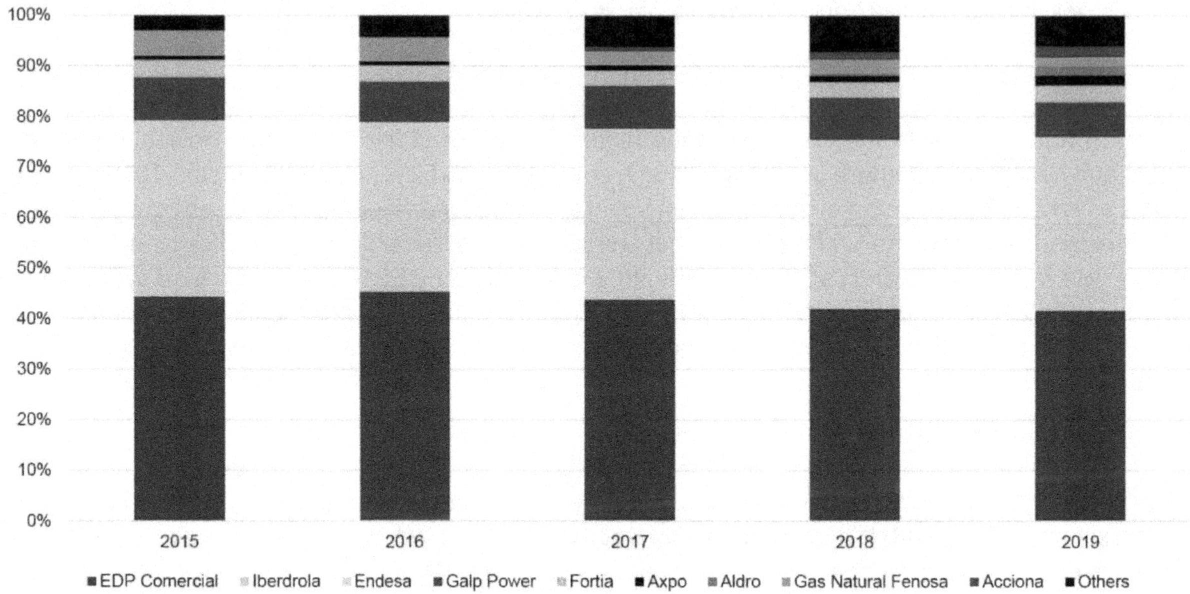


Source: (ERSE, 2020[12]).

*Natural gas market and key institutions (mainland Portugal)*

**Gas supply and wholesale market:** The Portuguese market is supplied through the interconnection with Spain and by the liquefied natural gas (LNG) terminal at the Port of Sines, based on long-term gas contracts. In 2018, approximately 62% of the natural gas supply was delivered by the LNG terminal.

**Transmission**: REN Gasodutos is the operator of the National Natural Gas Transmission Network. It was certified by ERSE in 2015 as the TSO under a full ownership unbundling regime. The TSO has the responsibility of preparing the assessment of the national natural gas system.[4] Activities on the LNG terminal including reception, regasification and storage of liquefied natural gas are operated by REN Atlântico, a subsidiary of REN S.A. All these activities are performed through public service concession contracts awarded by the state.

**Distribution**: The gas distribution networks are operated by 11 DSOs,[5] which operate in exclusive geographical areas through regional or local concessions or license agreements. Nine of these are fully or partially owned by GALP Energia SA.

**Retail market:** Currently, about 97% of natural gas consumption[6] is in the liberalised market, representing about 1.2 million customers. Residential and SME consumers have until the end of 2025 to switch from a supplier of last resort, in an attempt to finalise market liberalisation.[7] At the end of 2018, 12 suppliers were present, all serving customers with a consumption less than or equal to 500 m³/year. The biggest suppliers by number of customers as at February 2020 are: EDP Comercial (52%), GALP (24%), Goldenery (11%), Endesa (7%), Iberdrola (5%) (Table 1.1).

### Table 1.1. Market share for gas supply in Portugal

By number of customers, 2020

| Gas (February 2020) | |
|---|---|
| EDP Group | 52% |
| GALP | 24% |
| Goldenergy | 11% |
| Endesa | 7% |
| Iberdrola | 5% |
| Others | 1% |

Source: ERSE (2020), Liberalisation of the natural gas market, Change of supplier, https://www.erse.pt/media/21wjbt1a/202002_ml_gas.pdf.

#### *Interconnections*

The common Iberian Electricity Market (MIBEL) is an initiative between the Portuguese and Spanish governments, aimed at better connecting the two countries' electrical systems (Figure 1.5). This results in greater interconnection capacity available for commercial purposes (MIBEL, 2020[13]). The MIBEL Board of Regulators reflects its specificity as energy trading market and comprises energy and financial regulators from Portugal and Spain: ERSE and its Spanish counterpart (CNMC) for energy; the Portuguese Securities Market Commission (CMVM) and the Spanish Securities Market Commission (CNMV) on the financial regulation side.

REN, in its capacity as TSO, is responsible for the operation and technical capability of the grid, together with its Spanish counterpart, Red Eléctrica de España. The transmission grids in the two countries are integrated. Management capacity is approved by the MIBEL board under the harmonised action rules specific to Portugal and Spain as per European legislation,[8] and any congestion is managed through a mechanism of market splitting.

Electricity producers can trade through MIBEL, in addition to bilateral contracts. MIBEL is structured as a spot and a derivatives market, with management provided by Operador do Mercado Ibérico de Energia (OMIE). The stock in OMIE is owned equally by the Portuguese and Spanish states, with divided responsibilities between the derivatives and spot markets respectively (Europex, 2020[14]). The derivatives market operates on a daily basis offering continual negotiation services for various derivate products[9] and recording bilateral operations.[10] On the spot market, participants execute transactions on the daily and intra-day market created through markets splitting in the Portuguese and Spanish sides of MIBEL (CNMC, 2019[15]).

The EU-wide target for the level of electricity interconnection is 10% by 2020 and 15% by 2030 (IEA, 2016[11]). This is on a favorable trend, reaching 89% of the 10% target in 2018. The interconnection has an important role in energy integration and in the enhancement of security of supply. It also constitutes an opportunity to integrate the renewable energy production surplus in the European market, thus maximising the Portuguese potential for electricity production based on renewables (EC Expert Group, n.d.[16]).

## Figure 1.5. Interconnection of commercial capacity

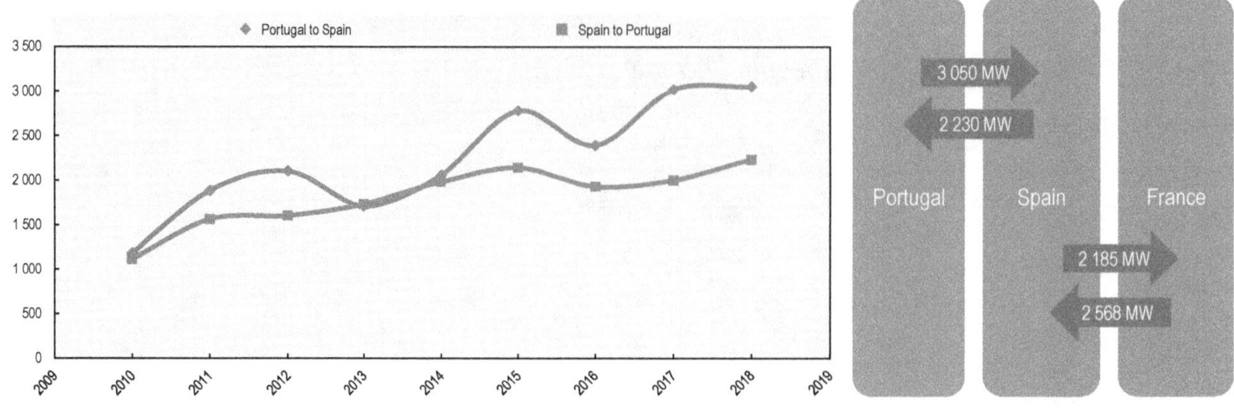


Source: NECP, DGEG.

During the 2nd Energy Interconnection Summit, the Lisbon Declaration was signed between Portugal, Spain, France and the European Commission (EC, 2018[17]). The declaration aims to strengthen regional co-operation within the framework of the Energy Union, and to better integrate the Iberian Peninsula into the EU energy market.

For natural gas, there is limited interconnection in the Iberian Peninsula due to more limited infrastructure.

### *Fuels*

ERSE is the regulator for the downstream fuels market, which includes petroleum-based fuels, liquefied petroleum gases and biofuels (Figure 1.6). The downstream supply is dominated by GALP Energia, the only operator capable of refining crude oil and which is vertically integrated with direct involvement in the wholesale and retail levels of the market. Other operators (BP Portugal, Repsol, Cepsa and Prio) are present in the procurement, logistics and retail sectors.

## Figure 1.6. Downstream operations in the fuels market

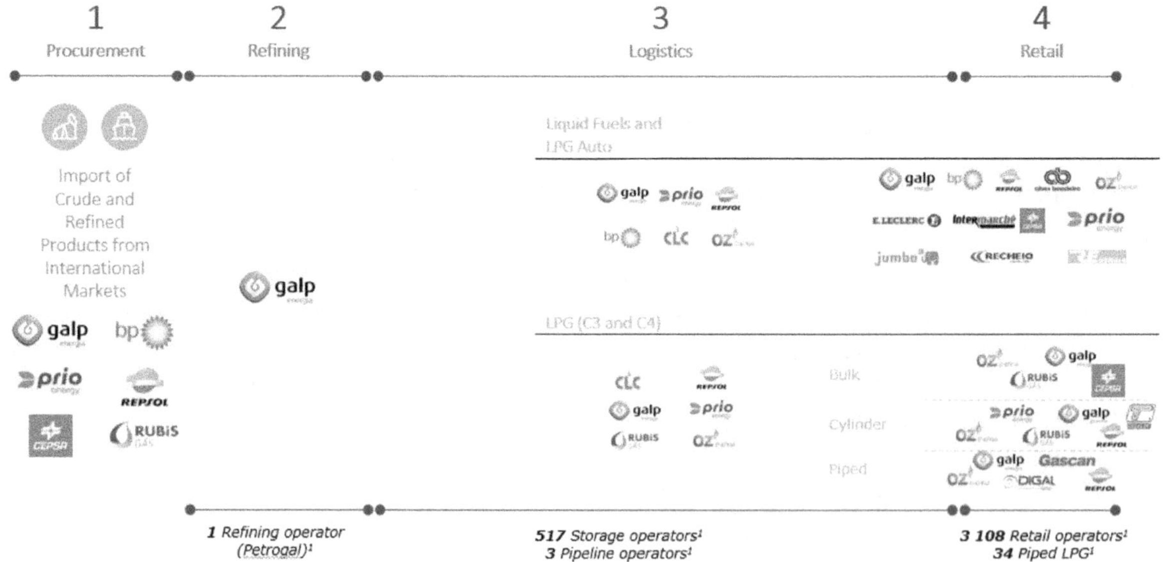


Source: ERSE.

### *Autonomous regions*

The autonomous regions of Azores and Madeira have responsibility for their own energy policy. The Azorean Directorate for Energy and the Madeira Directorate for Economy and Transport are responsible for adopting European and national legislation in the regional context, as well as issuing their own regulations, that take into account specificities of each region so that the energy system is secure, accessible and sustainable even in the most remote islands of the archipelago. They are also responsible for the licensing of all energy-related installations, such as those of the local electricity companies, filling stations or gas networks (Azores Gov, 2020[18]) (Madeira Gov, 2020[19]).

The energy sector in the autonomous regions is not liberalised. Two public energy companies – Electricidade dos Açores (EDA) in the Azores (EDA, n.d.[20]) and Eletricidade da Madeira (EEM) in Madeira (EEM, n.d.[21]) – are vertically integrated organisations responsible for the production, acquisition, transmission and distribution of electricity in all the islands of each archipelago. There is no natural gas supply to end-consumers on the islands. They are subject to both ERSE and regional authorities' regulation.

### *Tariffs*

ERSE sets tariffs for regulated activities of electricity and natural gas, network access tariffs and end user regulated tariffs.

End-user tariffs for electricity and natural gas in Portugal are composed of three components: network access costs, energy and supply costs, and taxes:

- network access costs comprise the fee set by ERSE and a second component, set by government in order to finance broader energy policies (such as cross-subsidies for the autonomous regions, subsidies for low-income households, feed-in tariffs for renewable energy, etc.);
- energy and supply component is regulated by ERSE for the regulated transitional end-user tariffs, and set freely for the market suppliers; and
- taxes are set by the Parliament.

Tariffs are set annually within a regulatory period that lasts three years for electricity and four years for natural gas. ERSE has the responsibility to approve the tariffs for both electricity and gas, and to publish and supervise compliance with the Tariff Codes. The codes establish the methodology used for calculating allowed revenues and tariffs and is preceded by public consultation.

As a consequence of the COVID-19 crisis, and for the purpose of providing stability and continuity to the electricity sector, ERSE extended the current 2018-20 regulatory period for the electricity sector until 31 December 2021.[11] ERSE's decision highlights that the current health crisis "entails such a dimension of unpredictability that, at this stage, it does not allow for the consistent definition of new regulatory goals and methodologies to take effect in a three-year horizon, i.e. in a new regulatory period" (ERSE, 2020[22]).

#### Tariff deficit

Tariff deficits represent shortfalls in revenues in the electricity or gas system, and result when tariffs for the retail electricity or gas price do not cover costs of generating (or delivering) electricity or gas to the final consumers. Portugal has a tariff deficit in the electricity market. Tariff deficits represent a mismatch between the integral electricity tariff (which should cover energy, network, taxes, levies, plus other costs) and the sum of corresponding costs incurred by energy utilities (IEA, 2016[11]). ERSE monitors the evolution of the tariff deficit and its impact on the economic sustainability of the electricity system.

Portugal's tariff debt is decreasing yet nevertheless remains a concern (Figure 1.7). In 2015, Portugal had one of the highest tariff deficits among EU countries. This arose in the aftermath of the last financial crisis, and at the time, it was estimated at EUR 5 billion, or approximately 3.1% of GDP (IEA, 2016[11]).

### Figure 1.7. Evolution of the tariff deficit (2007-2020)

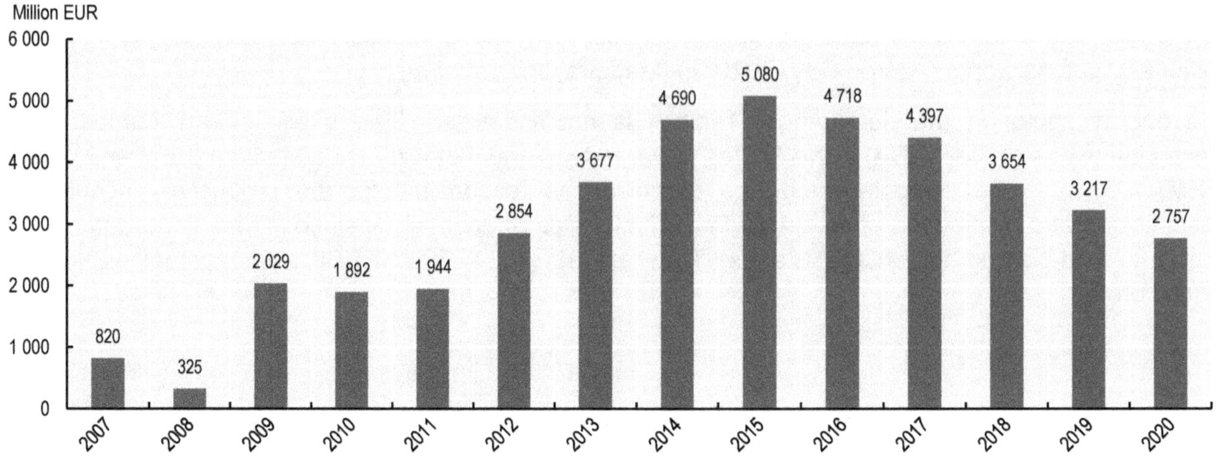

Million EUR

|  | Million EUR |
|---|---|
| 2007 | 820 |
| 2008 | 325 |
| 2009 | 2 029 |
| 2010 | 1 892 |
| 2011 | 1 944 |
| 2012 | 2 854 |
| 2013 | 3 677 |
| 2014 | 4 690 |
| 2015 | 5 080 |
| 2016 | 4 718 |
| 2017 | 4 397 |
| 2018 | 3 654 |
| 2019 | 3 217 |
| 2020 | 2 757 |

Source: ERSE, 2020.

## Key legislation

European Union legislation frames Portugal's energy policy (Box 1.1). EU policies in the energy sector are aimed at achieving a cohesive and integrated energy market, underpinned by competition in the generation, supply and distribution of energy. This policy framework is supported by a number of legislative pieces, the main one being the "Clean Energy for all Europeans" package, introduced in 2019, that seeks to promote the energy transition, to convey confidence to consumers and market agents, and establish clear regulatory rules (ERSE, 2020[12]). This legislative package follows the "Third Energy Package", introduced in 2009, which looked at matters around unbundling,[12] independence of regulators and cross-border co-operation (EC, 2019[23]).

### Box 1.1. European Union energy legislation, 2009 to present

#### 2009: The Third Energy Package

The European Union adopted the Third Energy Package in 2009. The primary aim of this legislative package was to aid in the completion of the internal European energy market. To this end, a number of measures related to the supply of electricity and gas were enacted:

- The unbundling of energy supply from network operators.
- The creation of independent regulators and the strengthening of their roles in the regulation of the energy markets.
- The enhancement of European regulatory cooperation through the creation of the Agency for the Co-operation of Energy Regulators (ACER).

- The strengthening of cross-border co-operation among the transmission system operators through the creation of the European Networks for Transmission System Operators for Gas and Electricity (ENTSO-G and ENTSO-E).
- The openness of retail markets and enhancement of consumer protection, including the ability of consumers to switch their suppliers, to receive information on their energy consumption, or to resort to efficient and cheap dispute resolution.

**2019: The "Clean energy for all Europeans" package**

In 2019 the EU completed an update of its energy policy framework. The "Clean energy for all Europeans" package comprises eight legislative acts. EU countries have 1-2 years to transpose the new directives into national law. The package aims to facilitate the transition away from fossil fuels towards cleaner energy and to deliver on the EU's Paris Agreement commitments for reducing greenhouse gas emissions.

It includes directives on:

- renewable energy, setting a binding target of 32% for renewable energy sources in the EU's energy mix by 2030.
- energy efficiency, setting binding targets of at least 32.5% energy efficiency by 2030 relative to a "business as usual" scenario.
- the governance system, under which each Member State is required to establish integrated 10-year national energy and climate plans (NECPs) for 2021 to 2030 outlining how they will achieve their respective targets.
- energy performance in buildings.
- electricity market design, comprising four elements: new electricity regulation, an amended electricity directive, risk preparedness regulation and a stronger role for ACER.

Source: EC (2020), Third Energy Package, https://ec.europa.eu/energy/topics/markets-and-consumers/market-legislation/third-energy-package_en (accessed 27 July 2020); EC (2020), Clean Energy for all Europeans package, https://ec.europa.eu/energy/topics/energy-strategy/clean-energy-all-europeans_en (accessed 27 July 2020).

The EU has set binding energy and climate targets for member countries to increase the share of renewable energy to 32%, and to reduce GHG emissions by 40% by 2030 (EC, 2020[24]). Countries must submit a 10-year National Energy and Climate Plan (NECP). Portugal's NECP includes a target for renewable energy of 47% of the national gross final consumption by 2030 (EC, 2018[25]).

## *Electricity*

On the national level, Decree-Law No 29/2006, of 15 February serves as the fundamental electricity law of the country, which establishes the general basis for the organisation and operation of the national electric system. This is complemented by Decree-Law No. 172/2006 on the regulation applied to the activities of electricity production, transmission and distribution and trading, the organisation of the respective markets and the procedures applicable to the access to those activities.

Transmission and distribution contracts are awarded to concessionaires, while generation and supply activities are liberalised. To prevent vertical integration, generation, distribution and supply activities are unbundled and legal separation applies (except for distributors supplying fewer than 100 000 customers).

### *Electric mobility*

On electric mobility, several legislative packages have been published in the past years, which now define the legal framework of the sector. European Directive 2014/94/UE created the framework for the creation of an infrastructure in the EU so that dependence on oil and gas is minimised, and also the environmental impact of transport is reduced. Decree-Law No. 90/2014 established the legal regime of electric mobility, together with the rules for the creation of a pilot electric mobility network. This was complemented by ERSE Regulation No. 879/2015, which covered rules for the exercise of activities related to electric mobility, and Ordinance No. 231/2016 (ERSE, 2020[26]).

The expansion of the laws and regulations was in sync with practical developments in the sector, which saw a continuous extension of the non-commercial phase of the electric mobility network. As of April 2019, public charging points are integrated in the electric mobility network and the costs of such loading are charged to the user.

### *Natural gas*

Decree-Law No. 30/2006, of 15 February is the fundamental gas law. ERSE retains responsibility for establishing the regulatory framework on access to natural gas infrastructure, including transmission system, distribution system, underground storage and LNG facilities. This is done through ERSE developed and enforced rules: code on access to the Natural Gas Network, Infrastructures and Interconnections (ERSE, 2019[27]). Further, third-party access to the gas infrastructure is offered on the basis of regulated access. ERSE sets the regulated tariffs that apply to them, and defines the methodology to calculate the tariffs in the Tariff Code.

### *Fuels*

In the oil sector, the main policy document concerns security of supply issues (the emergency plan for the mobilisation of oil reserves and petroleum products, so called PIURS was issued by the National Entity for the Energy Sector (Entidade Nacional para o Setor Energético, ENSE) in March 2019 (ENSE, 2019[28]). In addition, there was focus on the transposition of the European Commission Implementing Directive (EU) 2018/1581 of 19 October 2018 amending Council Directive 2009/119/EC as regards the methods for calculating stocks obligations, which was implemented in national legislation through by Decree-Law No. 105/2019 of 9 August. Furthermore, Decree-Law No. 69/2018 of 27 August, designated ENSE as the central stockholding entity in relation to stocks of oil and petroleum products, and added a number of responsibilities in terms of supervising and monitoring the energy sector.

## Notes

[1] EDP Distribuição changed its trading name to E-Redes on 29 January 2021.

[2] Portaria No. 83/2020 of 1 April. https://dre.pt/web/guest/pesquisa/-/search/130954976/details/normal?l=1 (accessed 17 September 2020).

[3] The new timelines in relation to the liberalisation process are as follows:

- for electricity medium voltage and special low voltage, the new deadlines are 31 December 2021 and 31 December 2022, respectively.
- for natural gas, the deadline for low pressure consumers with consumption above 10 000m$^3$ is 31 December 2022.
- for electricity standard low voltage and natural gas low pressure (i.e. household consumers), the deadline is 31 December 2020 and 31 December 2025 respectively.

[4] In accordance with the objectives and transparency requirements of Regulation (EC) 715/2009 of the European Parliament and of the Council of 13 July.

[5] DSOs operating under regional concessions: Beiragás, Lisboagás, Lusitaniagás, REN Portgás, Setgás, Tagusgás. DSOs operating through local natural gas distribution licenses: Dianagás, Duriensegás, Medigás, Paxgás, and Sonorgás.

[6] This figure does not include combined cycle power (CCGT) plants as customers.

[7] According to ERSE ordinance 83/2020.

[8] Commission Regulation (EU) 2016/1719 of 26 September 2016.

[9] This includes: futures, forwards, swaps, and options on baseload, peak and solar profiles, with physical or financial delivery.

[10] Over the counter (OTC) contracts

[11] Regulation No. 6/2020.

[12] The European directives provide for a departure from the vertical integration of energy companies, and instead propose a full unbundling of structures and functions. This is called ownership unbundling, i.e. independent operation and ownership of each of the energy system components: generation, transmission, distribution and supply. On the other hand, a number of operators have opted for legal unbundling. This allows for the structuring of activities under different legal entities with independent decision-making mechanisms, but nonetheless these entities can be owned by the same group.

## References

Azores Gov (2020), *Portal*, https://portal.azores.gov.pt/ (accessed on 4 December 2020). [18]

CNMC (2019), *Comparative Study of MIBEL Prices (Spot and Forward) with other European Markets and their Relationship with the Internal Energy Market*, https://www.cnmc.es/sites/default/files/editor_contenidos/Energia/Mibel/190703%20Resumen%20Ejecutivo%20Estudio%20Precios_EN_PUB.pdf. [15]

Commission, E. (ed.) (n.d.), *Modelling tools for EU analysis*, European Commission, https://ec.europa.eu/clima/policies/strategies/analysis/models_en#PRIMES (accessed on 4 December 2020). [7]

EC (2020), *Energy policy: general principles*, European Commission, https://www.europarl.europa.eu/factsheets/en/sheet/68/energy-policy-general-principles (accessed on 4 December 2020). [24]

EC (2019), *Third energy package*, European Commission, https://ec.europa.eu/energy/topics/markets-and-consumers/market-legislation/third-energy-package_en (accessed on 4 December 2020). [23]

EC (2018), *Second energy interconnection summit: Lisbon declaration is signed*, European Commission, https://ec.europa.eu/info/news/second-energy-interconnection-summit-lisbon-declaration-signed-2018-jul-27_en (accessed on 4 December 2020). [17]

EC (2018), *Summary of the Commission assessment of the draft National Energy and Climate Plan 2021-2030: Portugal*, European Commission, https://ec.europa.eu/energy/sites/ener/files/documents/necp_factsheet_pt_final.pdf (accessed on 4 December 2020). [25]

EC Expert Group (n.d.), *Electricity interconnections with neighbouring countries*, European Commission, https://www.consilium.europa.eu/uedocs/cms_data/docs/pressdata/en/ec/145397.pdf. [16]

EDA (n.d.), *Eletricidade dos Açores*, https://www.eda.pt/ (accessed on 4 December 2020). [20]

EEM (n.d.), *Empresa de Eletricidade da Madeira*, https://www.eem.pt/pt/inicio/ (accessed on 4 December 2020). [21]

ENSE (2019), *Documentação*, https://www.ense-epe.pt/reservaspetroliferas/documentacao/ (accessed on 14 December 2020) (accessed on 4 December 2020). [28]

ERSE (2020), *Annual Report on the Electricity and Natural Gas Markets in 2019, Portugal: Annual report submitted to the European Union, July 2020*, https://www.ceer.eu/documents/104400/6959701/C20_NR_Portugal_EN.pdf/296a59a1-a18a-a5a3-70d0-73ceedb579b2. [12]

ERSE (2020), *Annual Report on the Electricity and Natural Gas Markets in 2019: Portugal*, https://www.erse.pt/media/4nopbgnn/relat%C3%B3rio-ce-2019_en.pdf (accessed on 2 December 2020). [29]

ERSE (2020), *Gestão da mobilidade elétrica*, https://www.erse.pt/atividade/regulamentos-mobilidade-eletrica/gestao-da-mobilidade-eletrica/ (accessed on 3 December 2020). [26]

ERSE (2020), *Regulamento Nº 6/2020: Aditamento ao Regulamento Tarifário do setor elétrico*, https://www.erse.pt/media/wenf52kc/regulamento-erse-6-2020.pdf (accessed on 2 December 2020). [22]

ERSE (2019), *Regulamento de Acesso às Redes, às Infraestruturas e às Interligações*, https://www.erse.pt/ebooks/regulamentos-manuais-guias/gas-natural/regulamento-acesso-as-redes-rarii-gn-abril-2019/ (accessed on 3 December 2020). [27]

Europex (2020), *OMIE: Operador do Mercado Ibérico de Energia*, https://www.europex.org/members/omie/ (accessed on 3 December 2020). [14]

Eurostat (2020), *Market share of the largest generator in the electricity market: annual data*, https://appsso.eurostat.ec.europa.eu/nui/show.do?dataset=nrg_ind_331a&lang=en (accessed on 3 December 2020). [10]

Eurydice (2019), *Main Executive and Legislative Bodies*, https://eacea.ec.europa.eu/national-policies/eurydice/content/main-executive-and-legislative-bodies-60_en?cookies=disabled (accessed on 4 December 2020). [1]

IEA (2020), *IEA World Energy Statistics and Balances*, https://www.iea.org/data-and-statistics?country=WORLD&fuel=Energy%20supply&indicator=TPESbySource. [9]

IEA (2016), *Energy Policies of IEA Countries: Portugal 2016*, Energy Policies of IEA Countries, OECD Publishing, Paris, https://dx.doi.org/10.1787/9789264243637-en. [11]

IEEFA (2020), *Portugal to replace last coal plants in 2023 with hydro power complex*, https://ieefa.org/portugal-to-replace-last-coal-plants-in-2023-with-hydro-power-complex/ (accessed on 4 December 2020). [2]

Madeira Gov (2020), *Governo Regional da Madeira*, https://www.madeira.gov.pt/ (accessed on 4 December 2020). [19]

MIBEL (2020), *Mibel Homepage*, https://www.mibel.com/en/home_en/. [13]

OECD (2020), *OECD environmental indicators: country profile - Portugal*, https://www.oecd.org/site/envind/portugal.htm (accessed on 4 December 2020). [3]

Portugal Energia (2020), *Portal*, https://www.portugalenergia.pt/ (accessed on 4 December 2020). [5]

Portugal Gov (2020), *Portal*, https://www.portugal.gov.pt/pt/gc22 (accessed on 4 December 2020). [4]

Union, E. (ed.) (2017), *Energy Union Factsheet Portugal*, https://ec.europa.eu/commission/sites/beta-political/files/energy-union-factsheet-portugal_en.pdf (accessed on 4 December 2020). [8]

Union, E. (2012), *Directive 2012/27/EU of the European Parliament and of the Council on energy efficiency*, European Commission, https://eur-lex.europa.eu/LexUriServ/LexUriServ.do?uri=OJ:L:2012:315:0001:0056:en:PDF. [6]

# 2 Governance of the Energy Services Regulatory Authority

The Performance Assessment Framework for Economic Regulators (PAFER) was developed by the OECD to help regulators assess their own performance. The PAFER structures the drivers of performance along an input-process-output-outcome framework. This chapter applies the framework to the governance of Portugal's Energy Services Regulatory Authority (ERSE) and reviews the existing features, the opportunities and challenges faced by ERSE.

## Role and objectives

The Energy Services Regulatory Authority (*Entidade Reguladora dos Serviços Energéticos*, ERSE) is Portugal's regulatory authority for the electricity, natural gas and fuel sectors and the electric mobility network. It was created by Decree Law 187/95 as the Regulatory Entity of the Electric Sector in tandem with the liberalisation of the Portuguese electricity sector, and started its operations at the beginning of 1997. Its activity is most developed in the fields of electricity and natural gas regulation, given the breadth of European legislation that has been adopted for these sectors over the last 25 years.

### *Mandate and objectives*

ERSE's mandate and objectives are defined in legislation under article 3 of Decree-Law No. 97/2002, of 12 April.[1] Its main objectives are to:

- Protect the rights and interests of consumers, in particular economically vulnerable consumers, in relation to prices, quality of service, information-sharing, clarification and training;
- Guarantee conditions that enable economic and financial balance of the activities of regulated sectors carried out under a public service regime;
- Contribute to the progressive improvement of the economic, qualitative, technical and environmental conditions of the regulated sectors, encouraging, in particular, the adoption of practices that promote energy efficiency and service quality;
- Ensure compliance of regulated entities with public service obligations and other obligations established in the law and associated regulations;
- Promote and ensure competition between market players;
- Promote the resolution of disputes that may arise between regulated entities, through mediation and conciliation;
- Promote arbitration between operators and consumers, in accordance with applicable legislation, with a view to resolving disputes.

### *Mission, vision and values*

ERSE defines its mission, vision and values in its strategic plan 2019-2022 (ERSE, 2019[1]).

The current vision is "*to create value for society through an independent, transparent and sustainable regulation of the energy sector, by promoting the efficiency of the markets and by strengthening consumer confidence*".

The current mission statement is "*to regulate electricity, natural gas, liquefied petroleum gas, oil derivatives fuels and biofuels sectors as well as manage the electric mobility network, in defence of the public interest and to protect the rights and interests of energy consumers*".

ERSE's values were first set in 2002 and have remained fairly constant since. They are:

- Excellence
- Transparency
- Independence
- Co-operation
- Sustainability

## *Functions and powers*

Since its establishment as the Electricity Sector Regulatory Authority in 1995, the law has expanded the regulator's scope of activity several times. The regulator was renamed the Energy Services Regulatory Authority in 2002, accompanying an expansion of its mandate to the regulation of natural gas.[2] In 2012, ERSE's mandate was extended to certain responsibilities concerning the electric mobility grid[3] and, in 2013, to manage the electric mobility network operations.[4] In 2018, ERSE's mandate expanded to include a purview in the fuels sector, spanning the liquefied petroleum gas (LPG) sector in all its forms (namely bottled, piped and in bulk), oil-derived fuels and biofuels.[5]

ERSE's powers (defined in article 8 of the Decree Law 76/2019) include:

- Regulatory functions, including binding decisions
- Tariff-setting
- Advisory functions
- Mediation
- Supervision
- Sanctioning

*Regulatory functions*

ERSE prepares and approves codes and regulations that are necessary for the performance of its duties and that apply the legislation that governs the organisation and operation of the sectors that fall within its regulatory scope (Box 2.1).[6] ERSE may approve other regulations in addition to those set out in Box 2.1. The ERSE Board of Directors approve all codes and regulations after consultation with the relevant ERSE advisory councils and the public.

### Box 2.1. ERSE's regulatory functions by sector

**Electricity**

Within the scope of the electricity sector, ERSE is responsible for the preparation and approval of the following regulations:

- Regulation on access to networks and interconnections;
- Regulation on commercial relations;
- Tariff regulation;
- Regulation on quality of service;
- Regulation on network operations.

**Natural gas**

With regard to the natural gas sector, it is responsible for the preparation and approval of the following regulations:

- Regulation on access to networks, infrastructures and interconnections;
- Regulation on commercial relations;
- Tariff regulation;
- Regulation on quality of service;
- Regulation on operation of infrastructures.

**Fuels**

With regard to the fuels sector, ERSE is responsible for the preparation and approval of the following regulations:

- Regulation of storage, collecting and exchanging LPG bottles;
- Regulation on market operators' compliance with the obligation to inform the consumer of petroleum fuels and LPG;
- Regulation on Commercial Relations for piped LPG;
- Regulation on Quality of Service for piped LPG;
- Tariff Regulation for piped LPG;
- Regulation on the Quality of Supply of Fuels.

**Electric mobility**

Within the scope of the electric mobility sector, ERSE is responsible for the preparation and approval of the Electric Mobility Regulation.

Source: Information provided by ERSE, 2019.

Within its regulatory functions, ERSE has the power to guarantee third-party access to infrastructure. The regulator establishes the technical and commercial conditions for access to networks and interconnections in the electricity and gas sectors, as well as the remuneration to which entities are entitled for providing access to their networks. Access to piped LPG networks is foreseen in the National Petroleum System legislation and the regulatory powers are within ERSE's competences.

ERSE implemented in the past years four pilot projects,[7] as part of the process of advancing its strategic objective of "promoting clear, effective and dynamic regulation of natural monopolies". A few other initiatives are in train to be developed and launched.

### *Tariff setting*

In the electricity and natural gas sectors, the regulator defines the methodologies and sets tariffs and the allowed revenues of market actors in monopoly activities, such as transmission, distribution and supplier of last resort. ERSE sets tariffs within the framework of the law and of tariff regulations and ensures their application. Tariff setting for piped LPG networks is foreseen in the National Petroleum System legislation and the regulatory powers are within ERSE's competences.

The procedures for allocating costs by different activities are defined by the operators and approved by ERSE.

In addition, within its responsibilities to supervise compliance with unbundling provisions, ERSE establishes requirements on the granularity and disaggregation of the reported accounting information and evaluates the accounts reported by the companies.

### *Advisory functions*

ERSE contributes to the formulation and refinement of policies, laws and regulations. Its statutes set out its responsibility to provide advice and opinions on legislative initiatives or other initiatives in the energy sector to the parliament and the government.[8] ERSE also provides non-binding opinions to other public authorities, such as the Competition Authority, the Directorate-General for Energy and Geology (DGEG), the Directorate-General for Consumer Affairs and the Securities Market Commission (CMVM), as well the courts, on issues in the sectors under its remit.[9]

### *Mediation*

ERSE is responsible for mediating disputes between regulated companies and between regulated companies and their customers. Several other bodies can also intervene to attempt to resolve disputes between regulated entities and their customers, including arbitration centres and private consumer associations (see section on *Consumer protection* for more detail).

### *Supervision*

ERSE monitors and supervises regulated agents' practices and their compliance with relevant laws and regulations. To carry out its supervisory functions, ERSE has the power to:

- issue orders, instructions and recommendations within the framework of the applicable law and regulations
- grant authorisations and approvals
- enforce laws and regulations and other applicable rules within the scope of its powers
- request all the information it needs from regulated entities to exercise its powers and duties[10]
- conduct investigations, enquiries or audits of regulated bodies, upon its own initiative or upon a request from the member of the government responsible for energy[11]

### *Sanctioning*

ERSE has sanctioning power over some but not all of the sectors that it regulates and different legal regimes cover the sanctioning power of ERSE in the sectors under its purview.[12] ERSE is responsible for processing and sanctioning administrative infringements of legislation in the electricity and natural gas sectors under the Energy Sector Sanctions Framework. ERSE can impose a warning, a fine, accessory sanctions (prohibition of the exercise of any activity within the scope of the regulated sectors, prohibition of the exercise of an administrative or management position in entities intervening in the regulated sectors[13] (see section on *Enforcement* for more detail).

The Energy Sector Sanctions Framework has not yet been updated to include the implementation of the EU Regulation on Wholesale Energy Market Integrity and Transparency ("REMIT") which gives ERSE supervisory responsibilities to detect insider trading and market manipulation. Neither has it been updated to encompass the electric mobility sector; ERSE therefore does not have sanctioning powers over the electric mobility sector.

Fuels are subject to ERSE's sanctioning powers although this does not arise from the Energy Sector Sanctions Framework. Fuels, as well as the other sectors, are subject to other special regimes, e.g. the Complaint Book sanctioning regime and the Unfair Commercial Practices sanctioning regime (See section on *Enforcement* for more detail).[14]

## ***Co-ordination with other entities***

ERSE co-ordinates with a large number of other public and private entities in the course of its duties (Table 2.1). Some degree of co-ordination is provided for in legislation. Notably, ERSE is required to issue opinions (usually non-binding) to other bodies of the public administration, especially the Competition Authority, the Directorate-General for Energy and Geology (DGEG), the Directorate-General for Consumer Affairs, and the financial regulator the Securities Market Commission (CMVM).[15]

There are no permanent sector-wide formal mechanisms for co-ordination between the different actors in the energy sector in Portugal. However, the government does on occasion establish *ad hoc* groups on specific topics, depending on need, which appear to work well. ERSE participates when invited to take part in such working groups.

Similarly, there are no formal mechanisms at the national level to identify gaps in the regulatory framework or to assess potential overlaps between regulatory agencies. In some areas of regulation, a lack of clarity in the law or conflicting legal provisions might create conflicts between the mandates of ERSE and other entities. For example, different pieces of legislation give both ERSE and the National Entity for the Energy Sector (ENSE, *Entidade Nacional para o Setor Energético*) responsibilities for inspections and consumer dispute handling in the energy sector.

New legislation introduced between 2016 and 2018 redistributed fuel sector tasks between the newly established ENSE (previously the ENMC, National Entity for Fuel Markets), DGEG and ERSE. Before this, ERSE had no responsibilities in this sector, and all duties were carried out by ENMC and DGEG. ENSE became the stockholding entity for strategic oil reserves (previous role of ENMC) and also gained new responsibilities in terms of supervising and monitoring the whole energy sector (including electricity and gas), and some duties for inspections that were previously carried out by DGEG. DGEG retained responsibility for licensing and safety issues, while ERSE became responsible for regulating the downstream markets and for providing opinions on all the licensing activities of the National Petroleum System's infrastructures. ERSE ensures quality of service; promotes rules and the transparency of commercial relationships; promotes third party access to facilities declared of public interest and LPG piped networks and handles consumer complaints.[16] Regulation in the oil products and biofuels sectors relies to a large extent on *ex post* regulation, with the Competition Authority playing a major role until 2018.

ERSE's statutes enable the regulator to establish co-operation protocols with other regulatory authorities, universities, public or private research centres, as well as with institutions or general interest associations, such as municipalities or consumer associations. Taking advantage of this possibility, ERSE has established a number of (non-binding) agreements and protocols with entities with competences in the same sector as a mechanism of co-operation, to clarify the areas of intervention and to avoid duplication of activity.[17] For example, the regulator has established a co-operation agreement with ENSE specifically for the fuels sector as there is a degree of overlap in responsibilities for ensuring quality of service, commercial relationships and promoting third party access, given ENSE's previous responsibilities over this sector. The co-operation agreement seeks to resolve these overlaps for individual cases. In practice, this requires a case by case clarification.

In addition to co-ordination at the national level, ERSE carries out international regulatory co-operation and co-ordination. The regulator participates in the events and activities of the EU's Agency for the Cooperation of Energy Regulators (ACER), the Ibero-American Association of Energy Regulators (ARIAE), the Council of European Energy Regulators (CEER), the Association of Mediterranean Energy Regulators (MEDREG) and the Association of Portuguese Speaking Energy Regulatory Entities (RELOP).

ERSE is part of the Board of Regulators of the Iberian Electricity Market (CR MIBEL), which was created by an international treaty between Spain and Portugal. CR MIBEL is composed of the Spanish regulatory authorities for the energy and securities markets (CNMC – Comisión Nacional de los Mercados y la Competencia [energy] and CNMV – Comisión Nacional del Mercado de Valores [securities]; and the corresponding entities in the Portugal: CMVM (Comissão do Mercado de Valores Mobiliários) and ERSE. Draft regulation for the functioning of MIBEL, to be approved in Portugal or in Spain, are subject to the mandatory issuance of a non-binding co-ordinated statement of opinions by the CR MIBEL. The rules regarding the functioning of spot market are approved by Spanish authorities while the rules for the functioning of the futures market are approved by Portuguese authorities.

## Table 2.1. Co-ordination with other institutions

| Authorities | Mandate | Areas of shared competence with ERSE? | Formal co-operation in place? |
|---|---|---|---|
| *Public authorities* | | | |
| Directorate-General for Energy and Geology (DGEG) within the Ministry of Environment and Climate Action (MAAC) (*Direção Geral de Energia e Geologia; Ministério do Ambiente e da Ação Climática)* | Ministerial body for energy and geological resources, involving licensing and international relations<br><br>Contributes to the design, promotion and evaluation of energy policies<br><br>Participates in the elaboration of the legislative and regulatory framework<br><br>Electricity and gas:<br>• Supervises long-term security of supply<br><br>Fuels:<br>• Licenses operators and infrastructure<br>• Promotes third party access to facilities declared of public interest and LPG piped networks; ensures quality of service<br><br>Electric mobility:<br>• Licenses electric mobility suppliers<br>• Establishes technical requirements for charging points | *Electricity and gas*:<br>• Security of supply: DGEG monitors security of supply; ERSE monitors the evolution of installed capacity and the evolution of demand. ERSE issues a formal opinion to the government on network investment plans jointly with DGEG.<br><br>*Electricity*:<br>• Evaluation of PPEC applications (plan to promote efficiency in consumption): The evaluation of PPEC applications is carried out by DGEG and ERSE, with each evaluation weighing 50% for the final result. DGEG applies the rules approved by the Secretariat of State for Energy, concerning energy policy criteria, to be applied in the selection and ranking of applications submitted to the calls for tenders carried out under the PPEC.<br><br>*Fuels sector*:<br>• Promote third party access to facilities declared of public interest and LPG piped networks<br>• Ensure quality of service<br>• When investigating cases of breaches in laws or regulations in the National Petroleum System, ERSE maintains open dialogue with DGEG (as well as with ENSE and LNEG). | Legislation requires ERSE to issue opinions to DGEG when requested.<br><br>The evaluation of PPEC applications: co-operation is established in Portaria No. 26/2013 of 24 January.<br><br>Member of ERSE Advisory Council DGEG and ERSE participate together in the energy sector group for cybersecurity set up by the CNCS (National Center for Cybersecurity). |
| Directorate-General for Consumer Affairs *(Direção-Geral Consumidor, DGC)* | Ministerial consumer protection body<br><br>Oversees arbitration centres and supervises advertising<br><br>Receives and handles complaints | Handling consumer complaints in the energy sector | Member of ERSE Advisory Council |

| Authorities | Mandate | Areas of shared competence with ERSE? | Formal co-operation in place? |
|---|---|---|---|
| Competition Authority (*Autoridade da Concorrência*, AdC) | Promotes competition in all sectors, including energy | Promote competition<br><br>Promote rules and the transparency of commercial relationships | Co-ordination with AdC is included in ERSE statutes (Article 5)<br><br>When issuing a decision on merger operations involving assets or companies operating in the energy market, it is mandatory for AdC to obtain, according to the Competition Law, a non-binding opinion issued by ERSE, as the energy regulator.<br><br>When AdC launches an investigation for infringement of competition law, they inform the relevant sector regulator and ask for their opinion before issuing a decision; and vice-versa. |
| Securities Market Commission (*Comissão do Mercado de Valores Mobiliários*, CMVM) | Regulatory authority that approves rules involving financial products negotiation. | | MIBEL Council of Regulators (for electricity only) , based on an international Treaty between Spain and Portugal |
| National Authority for Communications (*Autoridade Nacional de Comunicações*, ANACOM) | Regulates the telecommunications sector. | Allocation of costs for the use of shared infrastructure between telecommunications and energy operators regulated by ANACOM and ERSE, respectively. | |
| National Entity for the Energy Sector (*Entidade Nacional para o Setor Energético*, ENSE) | Public corporation responsible for supervising and monitoring the energy sector.<br><br>Carries out inspection of the fuel, gas, LPG, electricity and natural gas sectors.<br><br>Creates, manages and maintains strategic reserves of crude oil and petroleum products. | Handling consumer complaints<br><br>Supervision, inspection and enforcement powers in the energy sector<br><br>Ensure quality of service<br><br>Promote rules and the transparency of commercial relationships<br><br>Promote third party access to facilities declared of public interest and LPG piped networks | Co-operation agreement<br>The objective of this agreement is to clarify each entity's role in overseeing the sector, in order to avoid conflicts of jurisdiction. The 2018 (and 2019) agreement was established in order to clarify the role each public agency would perform in the context of offences by sector agents. ENSE was tasked with overseeing and applying sanctions regarding the non-existence of a registry for consumer complaints in the establishments of electricity, natural gas and LPG, as well as fuel stations. Conversely, ERSE is tasked with overseeing the remaining offences in the same establishments. |
| National Laboratory for Energy and Geology (*Laboratório Nacional de Energia e Geologia*, LNEG) | Co-ordinates the process to ensure that biofuel sustainability criteria are being met.<br><br>Issues biofuel bonds.<br><br>Monitors compliance with the rules on promoting the use of biofuels. | Fuel prices: ERSE is responsible for publishing fuel prices, and LNEG is responsible for setting the incorporation targets of biofuels in road fuels. ERSE publishes the price of the biofuel incorporation in the final published price. | |

| Authorities | Mandate | Areas of shared competence with ERSE? | Formal co-operation in place? |
|---|---|---|---|
| Economic and Food Safety Authority (*Autoridade de Segurança Alimentar e Económica*, ASAE) | Monitors and ensures compliance with regulations governing the conduct of economic activities in the food and non-food sectors<br><br>Assesses and communicates about risks in the food chain | Enforcement of consumer rights in the energy sector.<br><br>On some occasions, given their wide remit, consumer rights cases may emerge that relate to energy markets, for example as regards "bundled products" which combine energy with services/products from other sectors (maintenance of household appliances or boilers, health insurance, etc.), as well as cases of unfair commercial practices and distance selling. The general EU legislation is implemented by ASAE. For the former cases, ERSE may be competent depending on the issue, for the latter, ASAE is always competent.<br><br>ERSE and ASAE also have responsibility for overseeing company call centres, depending on the issue.<br><br>In Portugal, companies are required to keep a "complaints book" for consumers. If located in the energy company, ERSE is competent, for other cases, ASAE is competent. | Memorandum of Understanding on joint areas of intervention |
| Portuguese Environment Agency (*Agência Portuguesa do Ambiente*, APA) | Manages $CO_2$ auctions | A portion of auction revenues is allocated to the national electricity system. ERSE is responsible for defining the tariff repercussion of these amounts. | |
| Portuguese Institute of Statutory Auditors (*Ordem dos revisores oficiais de conta*, OROC) | Establishes the technical standards for the certification of regulated accounts reporting | | |
| Tributary Authority *(Autoridade Tributária, AT)* | Handles information on the regulated asset base for tax purposes and tax flows for tariff reduction purposes. | Within 10 days of publishing the tariffs on the ERSE website, ERSE must report to AT the values of the regulated assets reported on 1 January, considered in the calculation of the definitive adjustments to the allowed revenues. | Defined in legislation:<br>Article 7(10) in Law 83-C/2013, of 31 December with subsequent amendments |
| Regional governments of Azores and Madeira | For energy, some competences of the national government are assigned to the regional governments (e.g. regional energy policy, investment planning).<br><br>The secretariats of the regional government are responsible for electric mobility. | Electric mobility | Members of ERSE consultative councils |
| Municipalities | Grant concessions for distribution of electricity in low voltage networks | Fuel sector: ERSE is responsible for providing opinions on the licensing activities of the National Petroleum System's infrastructures carried out by municipalities. | Co-operation agreement with the National Association of Portuguese Municipalities (Associação Nacional de Municípios Portugueses, ANMP) |

| Authorities | Mandate | Areas of shared competence with ERSE? | Formal co-operation in place? |
|---|---|---|---|
| Ministry of Environment and Climate Action (*Ministério do Ambiente e Ação Climática,* MAAC) | Sets national policy for energy and electric mobility<br>Responsible for security of supply of electricity and gas | | |
| Institute for Mobility and Transport (*Instituto da Mobilidade e dos Transportes IMT)* | Ministerial body for mobility and transport | Railway sector and the electricity sector: Several interactions related to topics involving the borders between the railway sector and the electricity sector | |
| *Private institutions* | | | |
| Arbitration centres for consumers (private institutions) | Consumer protection, provide arbitration (binding decisions) between consumers and operators in case of dispute | Handling consumer complaints in the energy sector | Co-operation agreements in place with the seven national and regional consumer arbitration centres regarding energy issues,[1] which cover technical support, training and financing |
| DECO (private association) | Consumer rights and advocacy organisation: Promotes consumer rights and handles consumer complaints, including in the energy sector | | Member of ERSE Tariff and Advisory Councils |
| IST, FDUL and FDUNL Universities | Research | | Co-ordination agreement (IST – Instituto Superior Técnico; FDUNL – Faculdade de Direito da Universidade Nova de Lisboa |
| *International* | | | |
| French Energy Regulatory Commission (*Commission de Régulation de l'Énergie,* CRE) | Regulates energy markets in France | ERSE must co-ordinate with CNMC and CRE, the Spanish and French regulators for energy to take decisions for the Southwest region, under the EU Electricity and Gas Regulations and any associated network codes, terms, methodologies and conditions of regional scope.<br><br>In addition, the regulators co-operate within the context of the European Regional Initiatives for electricity and gas, for the Southwest region, co-ordinated by ACER, which promote voluntary projects to reinforce regional harmonisation of the energy market, in line with the EU European Electricity and Gas Regulations. | EU Regulations and provisions relevant for the Southwest Region |
| National Commission of Markets and Competition (*Comisión Nacional de los Mercados y la Competencia,* CNMC) | Multi-sectoral authority, regulating energy markets in Spain | ERSE must co-ordinate with CNMC and CRE, the Spanish and French regulators for energy to take decisions for the Southwest region, under the EU Electricity and Gas Regulations and any ensuing network codes, terms, methodologies and conditions for the region. | EU Regulations and provisions relevant for the Regulation: Southwest Region |
| | | In addition, the regulators co-operate within the context of the European Regional Initiatives for electricity and gas, for the Southwest region, promoting voluntary projects to reinforce regional harmonisation of the region, in line with the EU European Electricity and Gas Regulations. | |
| | | Specific cross-border topics involving Portugal and Spain's common electricity | MIBEL Council of Regulators (for electricity sector only), based on an international |

| Authorities | Mandate | Areas of shared competence with ERSE? | Formal co-operation in place? |
|---|---|---|---|
| | | market (MIBEL). | Treaty between Spain and Portugal |
| | | Specific cross-border topics involving the construction of Portugal and Spain's common gas market (MIBGAS). | Although there is no treaty in place, MIBGAS is developed based on the EU Gas Regulation and EU network codes for gas, and following the signature between Spain and Portugal of a "Compatibility Plan for the regulation of the energy sector between Spain and Portugal," in 2007. |
| National Securities Market Commission (*Comisión Nacional del Mercado de Valores,* CNMV) | Regulates financial markets in Spain | Specific cross-border topics involving Portugal and Spain. | MIBEL Council of Regulators (for electricity sector only), based on an international Treaty between Spain and Portugal, signed in 2004. |
| Agency for the Cooperation of Energy Regulators (ACER) | Collects information on transactions on wholesale energy market which it shares with National Regulatory Authorities (NRAs). ACER generates alerts on potential market manipulation by market participants to notify NRAs.<br><br>Issues decisions, recommendations and opinions on wholesale market issues with cross-border relevance.<br><br>Promotes cross-border co-operation between the EU's national energy regulatory authorities.<br><br>Supervises the activities of the European Networks of Transmission System Operators (ENTSOs) for Electricity and Gas. | NRAs are responsible for conducting the investigations on REMIT breaches. If the REMIT breach involves more than one country, than the investigation must be conducted by the NRAs of those countries.<br><br>Apart from REMIT, under the European electricity Regulations there are, for issues with cross-border impact, a number of decisions which should be taken unanimously by NRAs. When that is not possible, decisions are escalated to ACER.<br><br>In addition, EU-wide network codes are developed and overseen by ACER, with input from the NRAs.<br><br>ACER also conducts annual EU-wide monitoring of wholesale and retail markets and consumer rights. | REMIT, the European Regulation No. 1227/2011 on Market Integrity and Transparency on wholesale electricity and natural gas markets.<br><br>EU *acquis communautaire* of legislation for the energy sector, namely the Third Energy Package and the Clean Energy Package for All Europeans. |

1. (ERSE, 2019[2]), Protocols, https://www.erse.pt/en/institutional/cooperation/.
Source: Information provided by ERSE, 2019-20.

## *Input into policy*

As noted in the section on *Functions and powers*, ERSE contributes to policy development through the provision of advice and (non-binding) opinions. This includes issuing formal opinions on legislative drafts, energy policy documents or other initiatives relevant to its mandate, at the request of the parliament or the government. Often, ERSE opinions include estimations of the economic impacts of measures, especially on regulated tariffs. Its opinions are made public via its website and in its annual report.

The government or the parliament can ask ERSE to present proposals or studies about the regulated sectors, in order to inform political decisions. Examples includes:

- A proposal about the terms and conditions of the new concession contracts for low voltage electricity distribution;
- Cost benefit analysis studies on relevant projects for the National Petroleum System's infrastructures, namely the pipelines for connecting the Sines Maritime Terminal of Liquid Bulks to the multiproduct pipeline between Sines and Aveiras de Cima, as well as a new storage facility for fuels and LPG in Sines, and the jet pipeline between Aveiras de Cima and the Lisbon Airport,
- A report about incentives on security of supply in the electricity sector).

The requests may be made by email, at a working level, but are generally made via a formal letter. The time that ERSE has to comply with requests varies, depending on the stage of the work of the government or parliament when they send the request. Inputs required by legislation usually specify deadlines of two to six months for ERSE to respond. Formal requests made by letter tend to have deadlines of two weeks to one month, and are not made public, but ERSE's response is made public. Informal requests made by e-mail have shorter deadlines (urgent or with about 15 days) and neither the request nor the answer are made public. These tend to be fairly specific requests, such as data simulation. The regulator reports that although the requests are manageable, they can become burdensome if several requests are made at the same time.

ERSE also issues studies and proposals of its own initiative, when it identifies market failures, with the goal of providing information and options to the legislator or the government (e.g. a proposal for the government to set maximum prices on bottled LPG during the State of Emergency declared due to COVID19 and a study by the Council of Regulators of MIBEL on the integration of renewable generation in the market).

ERSE may also participate in *ad hoc* working groups or expert groups established by the Ministry of the Environment and Climate Action (MAAC) to address specific policy issues. Examples include:

- Group to prepare the Roadmap for Carbon Neutrality 2050
- Group to accompany the Clean Energy Package legislative process
- Group to prepare the legislation on self-consumption of energy
- Participation in the jury for renewable (solar) auctions
- Group reviewing the legislation on the organisation of the natural gas sector

Depending on the working relations with the ministry, ERSE has been asked to provide technical views on international agreements and activities related to the energy sector, via the DGEG or directly to the ministry.

ERSE estimates that contributing to the formulation and refinement of policies, laws and regulations consumes about 10% to 15% of its total resources, mostly staff time.

## ***Strategic objectives***

### *Four-year strategic plan*

ERSE develops four-year strategic plans. In 2019, ERSE established a new strategic plan (ERSE, 2019[1]) for the period 2019-2022 that sets five strategic objectives. Under each strategic objective, ERSE has defined between five and six strategic priorities.

*Strategic objective 1: Fostering knowledge and the active participation of society in energy regulation and ensuring protection of the interests of present and future consumers*

*Priorities:*

- To combat energy illiteracy by promoting the training and information to consumers and other stakeholders regarding the energy sector;

- To ensure consumer protection in an environment of innovation and development of new services;
- To foster ERSE's external communication and adapt the contents according to the recipient;
- To innovate in the provision of relevant sector information;
- To strengthen public participation in regulatory decision-making.

*Strategic objective 2: Promoting efficient regulation of natural monopolies, in a context of decentralisation and innovation*

*Priorities:*

- To assess impacts and strengthen the rationale of regulatory decisions
- To promote the establishment of access to networks and infrastructure in a transparent, non-discriminatory way inducing overall efficiency (technical and commercial)
- To promote the setting of allowed revenues based on the economic sustainability of infrastructure and on the creation of added value for consumers, in a context of decentralisation and innovation
- To promote economically efficient smart grids and related services, placing digitalisation at the disposal of consumers and society
- To promote an efficient tariff structure in a context of decentralisation and innovation
- To discuss methodologies for the regulation of natural monopolies with a view of their improvement in a context of decentralisation and innovation.

*Strategic objective 3: Improving the functioning of wholesale and retail energy markets, reinforcing trust and enabling consumer involvement*

*Priorities:*

- To contribute to the harmonisation and integration of Iberian, regional and European energy markets
- To promote clear and unambiguous regulation (better regulatory definition)
- To ensure a continuing supervision of the markets and the monitoring of regulatory obligations and consolidate sanctioning actions
- To promote the efficiency of the markets and implement a risk management culture (guarantees) in the regulated sectors
- To foster consumers' active participation and demand management

*Strategic objective 4: Promoting clear, effective and dynamic regulation of natural monopolies, facilitating the energy transition*

*Priorities:*

- To monitor compliance with legal and regulatory provisions, improving relations with consumers and companies and their processes of reporting to ERSE
- To promote a transparent, integrated and harmonised regulatory framework that ensures the complementarity of regulated sectors and a dynamic regulation through the development of pilot projects
- To promote energy efficiency in all types of energy
- To identify, foresee and influence new trends and developments in the energy sector
- To envisage sanctioning actions in a context of energy transition and incorporate those challenges in our work

*Strategic objective 5: Affirming ERSE's excellence*

*Priorities:*

- To improve internal communications and knowledge exchange
- To promote ERSE's co-operation with similar entities and other national and international institutions
- To ensure the development of human resources, by promoting training and adaptation to new challenges
- Orientation towards a culture of planning and management, adopting control and monitoring tools for the activities carried out at ERSE
- Orientation towards a culture of information security and personal data protection
- Affirming ERSE's social concerns, namely in the involvement in social causes and in environmental sustainability

#### *Process for setting strategic objectives*

The strategic objectives for the period 2019-2022 arose from a process between the Board of Directors and all ERSE staff. This process kicked-off with a two-day workshop led by an external facilitator in which all the directors brainstormed about ERSE's strategic objectives. These objectives were then presented, discussed and approved by the Board. After this first event, each division organised internal meetings to discuss and set the priorities for each strategic objective.

Meetings were then held with the directors in order to collect contributions from all divisions and define ERSE's priorities. The main issues were identified and regrouped by themes and areas. The Advisory Council and the Sole Auditor delivered their opinions on the strategic plan. At the end of this process, ERSE's priorities for 2019-2022 were established and adopted by the Board.

ERSE is in the process of defining key performance indicators (KPIs) for the first time. KPIs are being defined by strategic objective or priority and ERSE will use the indicators to evaluate the implementation of the strategic plan. The process started with a request to divisions to define relevant KPIs. The divisions collectively produced around 300 indicators, and the Support to the Board (GACA) division will now merge and reduce the number. The division will also appoint a person to monitor the KPIs. The definition of KPIs was not imposed by legislation or agreements.

### *Independence and preventing undue influence*

ERSE's independence is enshrined in its statutes (Article 58) and under the Framework Law of Independent Administrative Entities. All regulatory entities in Portugal are legal persons of public law[18] having the nature of independent administrative entities that, in order to carry out their duties independently, must comply with the following requirements:

- Have administrative and financial autonomy
- Have management autonomy
- Have organic, functional and technical independence
- Have its own bodies, services, personnel and assets
- Have powers to issue regulations, regulate, supervise, and sanction infringements
- Ensure the protection of the rights and interests of consumers

### *Relations with government*

Without prejudice to its functional independence, ERSE must keep the government informed of its regulatory activity. ERSE should report in particular on recommendations, legislative proposals and draft external regulations which it intends to adopt, as well as on instruments in the framework of the government's general policy for regulated sectors.[19] ERSE informs in writing the member of the government responsible for energy of the launch of public consultations, of the submission of the tariff proposal to the respective Tariff Councils, as well as of the approval of the tariff regulation and tariff decisions. Similarly, ERSE informs the member of the government responsible for energy of ERSE's opinions on legislative proposals it receives for an opinion.

The government defines broad energy policy guidelines which ERSE must take into account, in particular on issues related to security of supply, protection of consumer rights, negotiation and conclusion of international agreements in the field of energy, energy efficiency, environmental sustainability and sustainability of regulated sectors.

Some of ERSE's activities are subject to ministerial approval by law and according to its statutes. The following documents are subject to approval by government (first the Ministry of Environment and Climate Action followed by the Ministry of Finance):

- Annual budget and the respective multiannual plan
- Balance sheet
- Annual reports and accounts

Due to the legacy of austerity measures, ERSE – like all Portuguese public entities including all sector regulators – is subject to controls on human resources and budget (see *Inputs* section for more detail). In practice, these controls may limit ERSE's management autonomy and reduce its agility.

### *Fostering a culture of independence*

Several measures are in place to foster a culture of independence internally. Article 10 of ERSE's internal code of ethics provides that its staff are bound by the principle of independence, and must respect ERSE's instructions and guidelines. Articles 29 and 54(5) of ERSE's statutes deal with incompatibilities and conflicts of interests. For instance, every year all staff members must sign a document to declare that they are not involved in a situation that could imply a potential conflict of interest. Should there be a potential conflict of interest, the employee must declare the information in writing to their supervisor.

In addition, the ERSE Plan for the Prevention of Risks of Corruption and Related Infractions,[20] in place since February 2015, requires an assessment of corruption risks in the context of the activities performed by the divisions and the adoption of relevant measures to mitigate the identified risks.

Press coverage shows that ERSE's independence has occasionally been questioned, including by parliamentary groups. For example, high energy costs became the subject of public and political debate in 2018. In response, Parliament convened a parliamentary inquiry committee. Over the course of a year, the committee heard from all of the ERSE presidents (past and present), ministers and secretaries of state (past and present), policymakers, competition regulators, presidents of the largest energy companies, presidents of industry associations and energy specialists.

## Input

### *Financial resources*

The vast majority – 95% – of ERSE's income comes from contributions (fees) paid by concession holders of the electricity and gas transmission networks,[21] which are included in the network access tariffs paid by consumers (Table 2.2). ERSE sets the level of the fees according to criteria that are defined in legislation.[22]

Since the expansion of the regulator's responsibilities in 2018, ERSE also receives revenue from operators in the fuels sector.[23] This contribution is based on the quantities of oil, gasoline and liquefied petroleum gases (LPG) introduced in the national market, which is determined on a quarterly basis and transferred to ERSE by the operators. In 2019, ERSE received four months' worth of revenues, which amounted to around EUR 240 000. For 2020, a complete year, the fuels contribution was forecast to represent about 10% of ERSE's budget. However, due to the decrease in fuels consumption during the COVID19 crisis, this percentage may not be reached.

The regulator also receives minimal revenues from fines (ERSE retains 40% of the fines from regulated entities). This amount has averaged EUR 189 000 per year over the last four years, although it can fluctuate significantly year to year. ERSE does not receive any income from the central government budget. However, ERSE's budget is integrated in the overall annual state budget that is approved by the Ministry of Finance and presented to parliament.

### Table 2.2. ERSE sources of revenue

| Source of revenue | 2016 | | 2017 | | 2018 | | 2019 | |
|---|---|---|---|---|---|---|---|---|
| | Amount | % of total funding | Amount | % of total funding | Amount | % of total funding | Amount | % of total funding |
| Contributions (Electricity) | 6 428 420 | 64.8 | 6 228 287 | 63.7 | 6 434 796 | 60.3 | 6 632 563 | 57.7 |
| Contributions (Gas) | 3 311 610 | 33.4 | 3 503 412 | 35.8 | 3 779 166 | 35.4 | 4 421 709 | 38.5 |
| Contributions (Oil) | 0 | 0.0 | 0 | 0.0 | 0 | 0.0 | 239 828 | 2.1 |
| Fines | 113 000 | 1.1 | 32 920 | 0.3 | 422 230 | 4.0 | 188 053 | 1.6 |
| Interest | 11 436 | 0.1 | 0 | 0.0 | 0 | 0.0 | 0 | 0.0 |
| EU Institutions (SAMA) | 45 739 | 0.5 | | 0.0 | 0 | 0.0 | 0 | 0.0 |
| Others | 6 347 | 0.1 | 8 853 | 0.1 | 36 858 | 0.3 | 4 726 | 0.0 |
| | 9 916 552 | 100 | 9 773 472 | 100 | 10 673 050 | 100 | 11 486 879 | 100 |

Source: Information provided by ERSE, 2020.

#### *Process for setting fees*

Once ERSE's budget has been approved, its fees are shared between the concession holders of the electricity and gas transmission networks, which has an impact on the tariffs that are fixed annually and borne by electricity and gas consumers. The calculation takes into account the number of customers and energy consumption in each of the networks (electricity and gas, respectively) from the previous year.

Unlike ERSE's financial independence in defining the contributions fees for electricity and gas, in the fuels sector the fee is determined annually by the government, on the basis of a formula established by Ordinance for 2019 and 2020, which ERSE then invoices to the relevant operators on a quarterly basis, as outlined above. The fees for the fuels sector are in practice subject to double approval by the government: in the first instance, the annual budget prepared by ERSE is approved by the Ministry of Finance and the member of the government responsible for energy; in a second instance, the two ministries issue the Ordinance setting the fee and formula for the fuels contributions for 2019-2020.The total contribution derived from the formula in the Ordinance in 2019 was significantly below that foreseen in

ERSE's budget. ERSE does not yet know how future fuels contributions will be calculated, from 2021 onwards, placing a degree of uncertainty on its regulatory and financial autonomy for these activities.

### *Process for setting fines*

ERSE sets fines in the electricity, natural gas and fuels sectors.[24] When determining the value of the fines, the regulator takes into account the financial situation of the regulated entity, the duration of the infringements, the regulated entity's compliance record and its degree of co-operation in the proceedings. Different processes apply according to the sector, which fall under different pieces of legislation:

- **In the electricity and natural gas sectors**, fines can be up to 10% of a company's volume of business in the case of very serious administrative infractions.
- **In the fuels sector**, ERSE has the power to impose penalties according to the Complaint Book sanctioning regime[25] and the Unfair Commercial Practices sanctioning regime[26] under the General Regime of Administrative Offences.[27] Under this legislation, fines may be up to EUR 44 891.81.

### *Managing financial resources*

ERSE's budgetary autonomy is enshrined in its statutes.[28] ERSE's statutes further specify that public accounting rules and the system of autonomous funds that apply to Portuguese public entities (including provisions on spending commitments, the carry-over and use of funds between financial years, and controls on budget disbursements) shall not apply to ERSE.

Despite this, subsequent legislation has curtailed ERSE's autonomy in managing its financial resources to a certain degree:

- In recent years, in some cases, a portion of the approved budget has not been released and cannot be spent without prior authorisation from the Directorate-General of Budget due to provisions introduced in the annual state budget. This practice has been named "*Cativações*" or "blocking". This practice also appears to be in contradiction with the Framework Law of Independent Administrative Entities[29] as well as the ERSE statutes. Independent legal opinion from two law firms has stated that this "budget blocking" should not be applicable to ERSE.
- According to ERSE's statutes, any budget surplus should be refunded to electricity and natural gas consumers in the form of a reduction on the network access tariff. The refund of the budget surplus is subject to approval by the Ministry of Finance. This has resulted in situations where the government has sought to retain the surplus for the state budget. The government recently took three former ERSE board members to court following their refusal to pass the surplus to the national treasury. In 2017, the former board members were convicted, after initially being absolved, to each pay a fine of EUR 2 550 and, jointly, to restore EUR 2 446 554 plus interest to the treasury.[30] ERSE complied with the decision.
- In accordance with ERSE's statutes and legislative provisions,[31] ERSE's expenditure is not allowed to exceed the approved budget. If additional funds are needed in exceptional circumstances, ERSE increase its income through charging fees or use of previous surplus, with the approval of the Government, or through developing an additional budget following the same approval process as for the annual budget.
- The annual state budget has occasionally imposed restrictions on public procurement, stipulating that spending on contracted services must have been foreseen as a budget item in the previous year.[32] These public procurement restrictions apply to all regulators and public sector bodies in Portugal. If ERSE wishes to foresee spending on procurement not foreseen in the previous year, it must seek approval from the Ministers responsible for Energy and Finance. Such budget line limitations could limit ERSE's discretion to implement new activities foreseen in its work plan or which arise in the course of the year.

### *Preparation of annual budget*

ERSE prepares its annual budget through the following process:

- Each year the Board approves the schedule for the preparation of the budget.
- Budget sheets and standard templates[33] are made available, along with underlying assumptions, through the ERSE internal portal.
- Each division makes a budget proposal that should reflect the activities agreed in the activity plan. The activity plan should already reflect the objectives set in the 4 year Strategic Plan.
- After collecting the proposals from each division, the General Administration Division prepares the consolidated document that is sent to the Board for approval. The board can change or reallocate budget but in practice this happens very rarely.
- The budget (and where applicable the multiannual plan) must be submitted for the opinion of the ERSE Advisory Council and the sole auditor.[34]
- The annual budget, the related multi-annual plan and the opinions of the Advisory Council and the sole auditor are submitted to the Ministry of Environment and Climate Action and the Ministry of Finance for approval within 60 days. The annual budget can only be rejected in very specific circumstances, such as unlawfulness or negative opinion by the Advisory Council.

Internally, the execution of the budget is monitored by the General Administration Division (DAG). Monthly budget execution is monitored using a dashboard which analyses the revenue by sector and the expenditure according to headings (e.g. personnel expenses, acquisition of services, IT investment etc.). The execution rate of the budget lines for each division is compared to the approved budget for the year. Each quarter, the DAG reports on the budget execution by each budget division. The reports are available to the Board and the heads of each internal division via ERSE's internal portal.

ERSE's expenditure is reviewed by the sole auditor on a quarterly basis. All receipts are subject to verification and any inconsistencies require a justification from ERSE.

Since the 2019 State Budget,[35] ERSE must comply with national accounting rules that are applicable to all public bodies in Portugal.

## Table 2.3. ERSE annual budget and execution

2016-19

| | 2016 | | | | 2017 | | | | 2018 | | | | 2019 | | | |
|---|---|---|---|---|---|---|---|---|---|---|---|---|---|---|---|---|
| | Budget | | Execution | | Budget | | Execution | | Budget | | Execution | | Budget | | Execution | |
| | EUR | % | EUR | % | EUR | % | EUR | % | EUR | % | EUR | % | EUR | % | EUR | % |
| Staff expenses | 6 430 618 | 66 | 6 035 034 | 62 | 6 706 190 | 69 | 6 479 909 | 66 | 6 894 469 | 67 | 6 478 629 | 63 | 8 132 876 | 66 | 6 939 339 | 56 |
| Acquisition of goods and services | 1 995 796 | 20 | 1 472 187 | 15 | 1 893 626 | 19 | 1 595 189 | 16 | 1 794 153 | 18 | 1 579 068 | 15 | 2 300 180 | 19 | 1 754 290 | 14 |
| Transfers | 616 208 | 6 | 620 147 | 6 | 633 608 | 6 | 613 547 | 6 | 666 752 | 7 | 668 237 | 7 | 846 231 | 7 | 786 664 | 6 |
| Taxes levies and expenditures | 9 549 | 0 | 2 003 | 0 | 10 252 | 0 | 2 893 | 0 | 10 082 | 0 | 3 589 | 0 | 10 738 | 0 | 11 794 | 0 |
| Capital acquisitions | 738 000 | 8 | 382 762 | 4 | 537 302 | 5 | 474 656 | 5 | 875 834 | 9 | 561 475 | 5 | 1 046 000 | 8 | 545 585 | 4 |
| **Total operating budget** | 9 790 171 | 100 | 8 512 133 | 87 | 9 780 978 | 100 | 9 166 194 | 94 | 10 241 290 | 100 | 9 290 998 | 91 | 12 336 025 | 100 | 10 037 672 | 81 |

Source: Information provided by ERSE, 2020.

### *Human resources*

Excluding its three board members, ERSE employs 95 staff, 80% of which are professional staff (Internally, the execution of the budget is monitored by the General Administration Division (DAG). Monthly budget execution is monitored using a dashboard which analyses the revenue by sector and the expenditure according to headings (e.g. personnel expenses, acquisition of services, IT investment etc.). The execution rate of the budget lines for each division is compared to the approved budget for the year. Each quarter, the DAG reports on the budget execution by each budget division. The reports are available to the Board and the heads of each internal division via ERSE's internal portal.

ERSE's expenditure is reviewed by the sole auditor on a quarterly basis. All receipts are subject to verification and any inconsistencies require a justification from ERSE. Since the 2019 State Budget, ERSE must comply with national accounting rules that are applicable to all public bodies in Portugal (Table 2.3).[1] The total workforce increased by over 20% between 2016 and 2019 as ERSE took on new responsibilities, for example in the fuels sector. Women make up 60% of all ERSE staff and one third of senior management roles (Table 2.4). Overall, turnover averaged 4% between 2016 and 2019, slightly higher than the turnover rate of government employees in Portugal which was under 1% in 2016-17.[2] Turnover at senior management levels was higher at over 11% on average between 2016 and 2019 (Table 2.5).

#### Table 2.4. ERSE workforce 2016-19

| Year | Number of support staff | Number of professional staff | Total workforce |
|---|---|---|---|
| 2019 | 19 | 76 | 95 |
| 2018 | 19 | 67 | 86 |
| 2017 | 17 | 64 | 81 |
| 2016 | 15 | 62 | 77 |

Source: Information provided by ERSE, 2020.

#### Table 2.5. ERSE workforce by gender, 2019

| Staff category | Male | Female | Total |
|---|---|---|---|
| Senior management | 4 | 2 | 6 |
| Technical staff | 28 | 42 | 70 |
| Support staff | 6 | 13 | 19 |
| Total | 38 | 57 | 95 |

Source: information provided by ERSE, 2020.

#### Table 2.6. ERSE turnover rate, 2016-19

| Turnover | 2016 | 2017 | 2018 | 2019 |
|---|---|---|---|---|
| Seniormanagement | 14.3% | 14.3% | 0.0% | 16.7% |
| Technicalstaff | 4.1% | 1.8% | 6.9% | 4.9% |
| Supportstaff | 0.0% | 0.0% | 0.0% | 5.3% |
| Total | 4.2% | 2.6% | 4.9% | 5.8% |

Source: information provided by ERSE, 2020.

ERSE makes use of contractors or external consultants for some functions. The use of contractors varies year to year, but in 2018 the share was around 20%. ERSE typically uses contractors for certain IT services linked to market monitoring, audits and external legal representation.

### *Staff composition*

As regards academic qualifications, the most represented fields in ERSE are engineering (24%), law (22%) and economics (22%), assuming a variety of tasks in different divisions. Other qualifications include management, finance, international relations, etc. In the context of developments in technology, the extension of responsibilities and expansion of EU level obligations where ERSE has important functions, directors stressed the need to strengthen the following areas and capabilities:

- knowledge about emerging concepts such as sector coupling and energy communities, circular economy and innovation, decarbonisation, the role of final consumers in market design and operation
- communication and support to market actors (especially in the context of new types of market actors/energy consumers entering the scene)
- behavioural science
- data management, big data analysis.

## Table 2.7. ERSE workforce by division, 2019

| | Board of Directors | Support to the Board of Directors | Support to the Energy Consumers | Communication, image & institutional relations | Costs and Revenues division | Infrastructures and network division | Markets and Consumers division | Pricing and Tariffs division | General Administration division | Legal division | National Petroleum System Installation Commission | **Total** |
|---|---|---|---|---|---|---|---|---|---|---|---|---|
| President | 1 | | | | | | | | | | | **1** |
| Board Member | 2 | | | | | | | | | | | **2** |
| Director | | | | | 1 | 1 | 1 | 1 | 1 | 1 | | **6** |
| | | | | | | | | | | | | |
| Senior Advisor | | 2 | | | 1 | 2 | | | | | | **5** |
| Advisor | | 4 | 1 | 2 | 2 | 1 | 2 | 1 | 2 | 1 | 1 | **17** |
| Specialist | | 1 | 3 | | 3 | 2 | 4 | 6 | 6 | 2 | 2 | **29** |
| Graduate staff | | 3 | 3 | | 2 | 1 | 4 | 1 | 2 | 2 | 1 | **19** |
| | | | | | | | | | | | | |
| Support staff | | 2 | 1 | 1 | 1 | 1 | 1 | 1 | 5 | 1 | | **14** |
| IT expert | | | | | | | | | 2 | | | **2** |
| Driver | | 1 | | | | | | | 1 | | | **2** |
| Receptionist | | | | | | | | | 1 | | | **1** |
| | | | | | | | | | | | | |
| **Total** | **3** | **13** | **8** | **3** | **10** | **8** | **12** | **10** | **20** | **7** | **4** | **98** |

Source: information provided by ERSE, 2020.

### Recruitment

Recruitment is carried out through open public competition in line with the *Code of Administrative Procedure*, ERSE's statutes,[1] and ERSE's internal regulation on recruitment (*Regulamento de Recrutamento de Pessoal da ERSE*). All job openings are advertised in a national newspaper, on the ERSE website and in the Portuguese civil service job portal. There is no legal restriction on ERSE's ability to recruit from the regulated industry for staff below Board member level. Since 2013, ERSE must secure government authorisation to increase the number of staff.[2] The approval process can be lengthy, taking from around six months to a year to create some posts. Job titles and profiles, however, remain at ERSE's full discretion.

To open a position, divisions must make a request to the General Administration Division (DAG). Together the DAG and the division define the job description, ideal candidate profile (CV requirements, etc.), interview questions and recruitment timelines. An internal jury is established for each recruitment process and the selected candidate is proposed to the Board for approval. The evaluation criteria are not standardised, but adapted to the specificities of each job opening. Once the chosen candidate has been confirmed, the final decision is not publicised beyond ERSE.

### Contract conditions

All staff are hired on a direct employment contract (i.e. not a public servant contract). Contracts are governed by ERSE's internal regulations and by the Portuguese *Labour Code*. The use of temporary or fixed term contracts is marginal (currently only one case), although ERSE does have a trainee programme for recent graduates whose contracts cannot be extended beyond one year. In addition, ERSE offers the possibility of "curricular" traineeships, for university studies who are completing a degree.

Directors and heads of division are appointed for a three-year period, automatically renewable for an equal period, unless one party advises the other party of their non-renewal. When the appointment ceases, the director/head of division can return to the career category they held at the time of appointment.

ERSE can also receive staff on secondment from the public administration, typically from ministries, and as at June 2020 it has 17 staff in this category. A legal framework for public administration secondments governs these arrangements. Although ERSE staff are not civil servants, regulatory authorities are able to apply the legal framework and receive staff from the public administration. However, secondments between regulatory authorities (e.g. water, telecoms, etc.) are not possible as staff in regulators are not civil servants according to the framework. Seconded staff retain their career progression in the public administration, and are entitled to choose between their original salary arrangements or the salary that corresponds to the tasks performed at ERSE. Secondments can be renewed or revoked at any time (with a notice period), with the individual returning to their home administration. There has not been any formal assessment of the arrangements but generally speaking it is seen to work well. Some staff have been seconded to ERSE for many years.

### Remuneration and career progression

Salaries are not linked to public servant bands but are set independently by ERSE. The flexibility in setting salary bands depends on the job function, professional experience and the academic background of the candidate. Some minor benefits, such as mobile phones and parking spots, are available to some positions. Otherwise, all staff benefit from the same employment package in terms of pension, healthcare, lunch vouchers, etc.

However from 2009, ERSE (along with all of the public administration and regulatory authorities) was subject to a national austerity policy that saw career progressions frozen and salaries cut. These measures began to ease from 2016:

- From 2016-2019 the regulator was able to gradually return salaries to their 2009 levels.
- In 2018, the Annual State Budget law allowed careers to be unfrozen, so that automatic progressions, promotions and recognition of years of service were again reactivated. ERSE has undertaken these corrections and updates for all staff. The 2019 Annual State Budget law nevertheless required government authorisation for promotions and performance-based bonuses. In 2020, this requirement was removed (via the 2020 State Budget). Promotions are thus possible and ERSE has accordingly proceeded to promote several of its staff, some of whom had not been promoted in over 15 years.
- Salary increases of 0.3% for the public administration were announced in 2020. Although not tied directly to public levels, ERSE approved a similar salary increase for its staff. The previous increase took place in ERSE in 2009 (1.2%). Prior to the austerity period, such reviews and increases took place annually.

Since March 2017, the maximum salary for Board members of all regulatory bodies is set by law at around EUR 8 300 per month plus representation expenses, leading to a significant reduction in the ERSE Board members' salaries. By comparison to the 2016 salaries, the reduction amounts to 31% in the case of the Board president, and 23% for the other two Board members. In theory, Board salaries cannot be lower than the most senior management position in the regulatory body, but in practice the upper salary level foreseen for the Director-General for Regulation (position currently vacant) would exceed that of the Board members.

Regarding the levels of remuneration relative to the energy sector, ERSE does not systematically review data on salaries.

### *Training*

ERSE has an annual training plan for its staff. Training is divided into several categories: *strategic,* relating to ERSE's regulatory activities (e.g. training on the regulation of energy utilities, the regulation and integration of renewable energy;...); *operational*, relating to staff functions (e.g. data analysis, econometrics, IT tools;...); or *transversal*, relating to general professional development (e.g. project management, communication, foreign languages, etc.). According to the ERSE training plan, in 2019, most of the training time was dedicated to transversal (>5 000 hours), followed by operational (~2 400 hours) and strategic (~1 200 hours).

Each division assesses its own training needs and submits requests to the General Administration Division (DAG). The DAG merges the requests, identifies efficiencies and priorities, and defines the annual training plan and budget in line with the overall available budget. The plan and budget are then sent to the Board for approval. The plan prioritises training for staff who have not had any training during the previous three years, in order to comply with the legal minimum set in the Labour Code of 40 hours per year per employee.[3] Each division is allocated the same budget for training, regardless of team size, requiring each division to prioritise accordingly. Training can also be offered to staff to award good performance.

### *Performance evaluation*

The system for performance evaluation, in place since 2008, aims to ensure that the objectives of all staff are aligned with the goals of the organisation. A guide to the system is set out in a manual that is available to staff on the intranet (*Manual do Modelo de Gestão de Desempenho*, June 2018).

Managers evaluate an individual's performance on an annual basis according to two components: goals and competences. Goals are set in a top-down fashion and linked to ERSE's strategic objectives. Competences are set by each division. Staff members can also give feedback on their head of division anonymously through a dedicated platform.

Career progression is linked more closely to length of service than to performance. As mentioned above, in practice, however, austerity measures imposed by law froze career progression between 2009 and 2018. Following their relaxation, since 2019 ERSE has applied the regime of automatic progressions and remuneration adjustments according to the legal provisions.

In parallel to automatic career progressions, ERSE leadership state that a lack of management tools to recognise good performance and promote meritocracy is a challenge. During 2019, the requirement of government authorisation for promotions and performance-based bonuses was a particular constraint, although this obligation was removed in 2020.

## Process

### *Governing body and decision making*

ERSE is headed by a three-person Board of Directors composed of a president and two members. The Board is responsible for defining, guiding and monitoring ERSE's activities and services, as well as representing ERSE and ensuring the performance of activities.[4] Its main duties are to:

- Set the strategic direction of the organisation and develop policy
- Monitor performance of the regulator
- Ensure compliance with the law, the organisation's statutes and policies
- Approve codes and other decisions that enforce regulation
- Take sanctioning decisions, including decisions related to the application of fines and additional sanctions
- Deliver formal opinions requested by other public bodies
- Deliver strategic plans, annual and multi-annual activity plans, the annual budget, annual accounts and activity reports
- Approve internal regulations
- Collect and manage revenues and authorise expenses
- Define ERSE's internal organisation and charts of the respective staff, undertake the recruitment thereof
- Exercise staff direction, management and discipline powers
- Administer contracts
- Represent the organisation with respect to national and international institutions, (e.g. EU) and/or appoint ERSE's representatives to other bodies or institutions
- Delegate

The President co-ordinates the activity of the Board and has responsibility to:[5]

- Convene its meetings and set the respective agenda
- Chair meetings, guide the work and ensure compliance with deliberations of the Board of Directors
- Represent ERSE in and out of court
- Secure ERSE's relations with parliament, the government and other public or private bodies
- Request opinions from the Sole Auditor, the Advisory Council, the Tariff Council and the Fuels Council
- Exercise the tasks delegated by the Board of Directors

The President can delegate the performance of part of their tasks to other members of the Board.

## Table 2.8. Composition of the Board of Directors

| Position | Board member | Member since |
|---|---|---|
| President[1] | Maria Cristina Portugal | 03/06/2016 |
| Member | Mariana Pereira | 15/05/2017 |
| Member | Pedro Verdelho | 01/02/2019 |

1. Maria Cristina Portugal was appointed ERSE President in May 2017, for the remainder of her 6-year mandate, having been appointed as member of the board in June 2016.
Source: ERSE, 2020.

There is a division of labour between the Board whereby each member oversees the work of particular divisions. Board members are highly involved in the work of their assigned divisions and meet weekly with the heads of division and teams.

### *Selection and dismissal of members of the board*

Legislation establishes that board members must have adequate qualifications, recognised independence, and technical and professional competence in the regulated activities. In addition, women and men must be represented at all times, with a minimum of one third representation each.

Board members are appointed by the Council of Ministers, following their nomination by the member of government responsible for energy and opinions from the Public Administration Recruitment and Selection Committee (CRESAP) and the parliament. CRESAP is an independent committee created in 2012 to review candidates for high level positions in central public administration bodies or equivalent. CRESAP issues a formal opinion on the basis of a candidate's curriculum vitae, their experience and the fulfilment of any incompatibility requirements. The candidate is then heard by the relevant parliamentary commission, which issues a non-binding opinion. The Council of Ministers then makes the final decision. Although the opinion of the parliamentary commission is non-binding, in practice, the appointment of a candidate to the ERSE Board was once rejected following a negative opinion from the parliament.

Appointments of board members must be staggered, with a minimum period of six months required between appointments. The term of office is six years, not renewable.

The criteria for dismissing board members from office are defined in law. Board members can only be dismissed before the end of their term in the following cases: permanent physical or psychological incapacity or with a predicted duration exceeding the date of expiry of the term of office; supervening incompatibility; conviction by a final and non-appealable sentence for a felony that calls into question their suitability to exercise the office; serving a prison sentence; the dissolution of the board, or the termination of ERSE.[6]

The dissolution of the Board and the dismissal of any of its members may only take place by means of a resolution of the Council of Ministers based on a justified reason, within a process led by an independent entity[7] and after considering the opinions of ERSE's Advisory Council and the parliament.[8] A 'justified reason' is a serious misconduct of individual or collective responsibility, corresponding to:[9]

- Unjustified failure to meet the ERSE aims for reasons attributable to the board or the member of the board;
- An excessive gap between the approved budget and its implementation, when the costs incurred unwarrantedly exceed the budget by 15%;
- Serious irregularities in the functioning of the body, considering as such the practice of serious or repeated breaches of the law or ERSE Statutes;
- Serious or repeated failure to comply with the laws and regulations applicable to ERSE and its guidelines;

- Failure to comply with the duty to exercise functions or serious or repeated breach of confidentiality.

Board members are subject to both pre- and post-employment restrictions. Pre-employment restrictions provide that board members cannot have been a member of any board or management body of any company directly intervening in the regulated sectors in the two years prior to their appointment. Furthermore, they cannot hold offices/appointments in the government or in the regulated industry while they are board members. However, they are allowed to have teaching and research duties.[10] After their term of office, Board members can only accept jobs in the regulated sectors after a two-year cooling-off period. Board members are remunerated during this cooling-off period.

#### *Decision-making process*

Board meetings take place once a week. The board uses a digital platform ("Portal do CA") to manage the decision-making process.[11] ERSE divisions submit relevant items for approval, information or review by the board via this portal. Submissions that require a board decision include a 'suggested decision' from the ERSE divisions, which the board can simply approve, or it may request further information or clarification from the relevant head of division before taking its decision. As such, the board relies greatly on the technical input from ERSE teams, and in particular the heads of division, in its decision-making.

All exchanges within the decision-making process (submissions, requests for further information/clarification, decisions) are recorded in the portal, although in practice board members will usually have discussed issues in person with the relevant head of division in the course of their regular meetings: the board holds a weekly co-ordination meeting with all heads of division and each member meets weekly with their assigned divisions.

Furthermore, the Support to the Board division is composed of a team of ten experts with different backgrounds, whose tasks include advising the board, co-ordinating cross-cutting activities (e.g. elaboration of strategic plan) and supporting the board on strategies and activities at the European and international level.

The board's decision-making is also informed by three independent, external bodies: the Advisory Council, the Tariff Council and the Fuels Council (see section on *Councils*) – provide non-binding opinions on all proposed regulatory decisions, for consideration by the board before it takes its final decision. In addition, the sole auditor provides the Board with interim and annual assessments of ERSE's financial and asset management from a legal compliance perspective, which also serve to inform the Board's decisions.

Decisions are taken by majority or by unanimous decision of the three board members. The president has the blocking vote. When the board takes a decision, the relevant head of division/manager is notified automatically through the portal.

ERSE publishes the non-confidential versions of its decisions and sends them to its mailing list and may publish them on its website. The minutes of its meetings are not published.

### *Internal organisation and management*

ERSE is currently restructuring. Under the new structure, ERSE will create several new divisions and reallocate some tasks and functions between existing divisions. The four new divisions include: an Internal Management Office (GGI) an Innovation and Special Projects Development Office (IDEP), an International Relations Office (GRI),[12] and the reinstatement of a Directorate General of Regulation. The position of Director General of Regulation, although appearing on the current organigram, has been vacant since 2017.

ERSE divisions are structured by function (e.g. tariff setting) rather than by sector, with the exception of a small team that was established when ERSE took on new responsibilities in the fuels sector. The organisation by function rather than sector will continue under the new structure.

All divisions and offices report to the Board.

### Figure 2.1. ERSE current structure

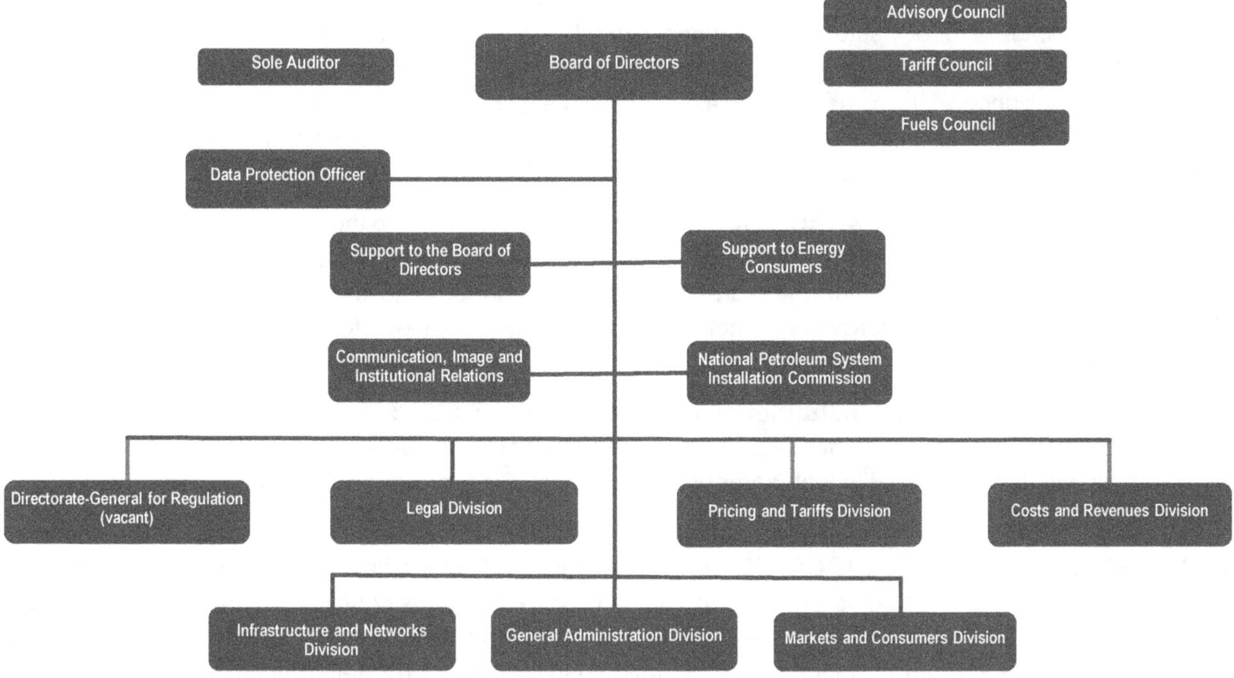


Source: Information provided by ERSE, 2020.

### Figure 2.2. ERSE's planned new structure, to be implemented from 2020

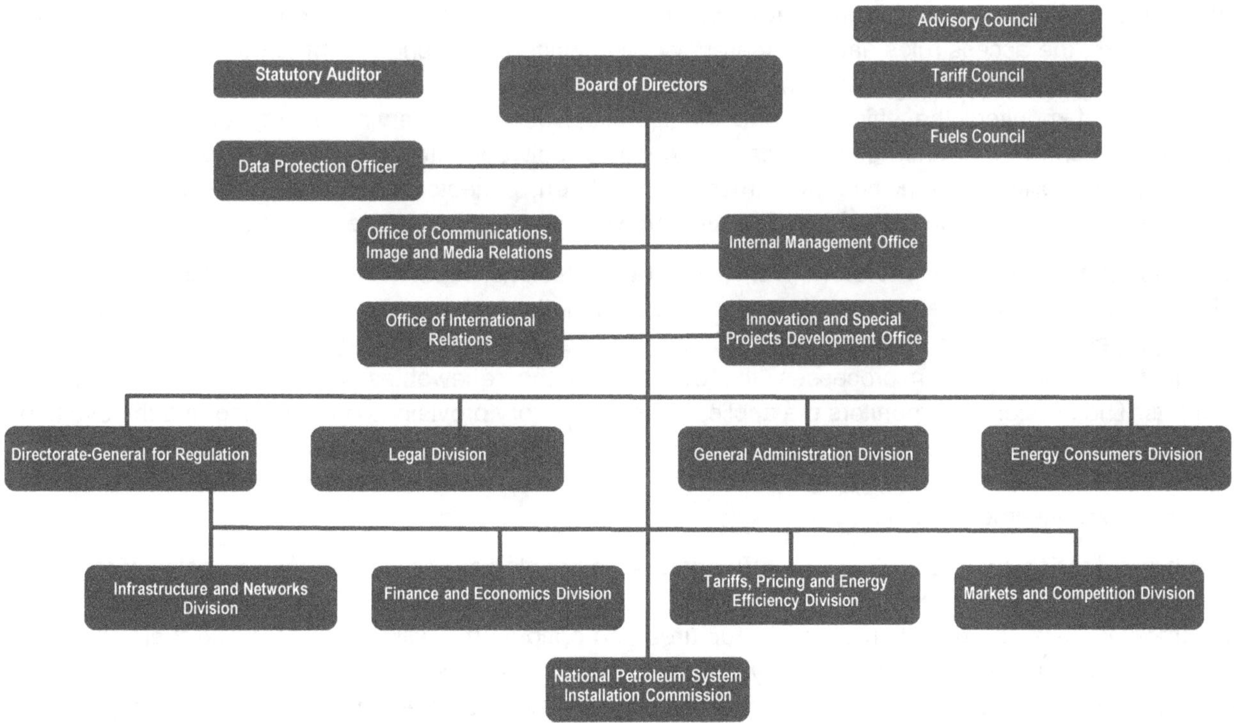


Note: New organigram to be implemented during the restructuring.
Source: Information provided by ERSE, 2020.

*Current teams*

**Support to the board of directors (GACA, 13 staff)**: This team provides support to the Board of Directors by preparing documents, co-ordinating outputs across different divisions and representing ERSE at different forums. In addition to providing the secretariat support for the Board, the team advises the Board on national and international institutional relations with other entities. Under the new structure, the tasks of this division will be divided between different teams: tasks of co-ordinating outputs that span several divisions or that concern the organisation as a whole (e.g. preparation of the strategic plan) will be undertaken by the directorate-general for regulation. International relations work will be undertaken by a new unit dedicated to this portfolio.

**Support to energy consumers (ACE, 8 staff):** responsible for analysing consumer complaints and promoting consumer rights. It also deals with the requests for information from energy consumers, legislative and regulatory protection measures and the instruments necessary for effective safeguarding of the rights and interests of energy consumers, including training sessions for consumer organisations. In the new structure, these tasks will be absorbed into the new Energy Consumers Division.

**Communication, image and institutional relations office (CIRI, 3 staff):** designs strategies and instruments for internal and external institutional communication. It drafts press releases and manages relationships with the media, edits web content and ensures ERSE's presence on social media/networks. This office will be maintained in the new structure.

**Costs and revenues division (DCP, 10 staff):** designs models for calculating allowed revenues of regulated activities. It defines adjustments for previous years, references costs and parameters associated with allowed revenues. It also analyses the evolution and economic and financial performance of regulated activities. It monitors the performance and economic sustainability of regulated sectors and companies, the economic and financial flows associated with fees, and the taxes or social support and investments and assets. Under the new structure, it will be renamed the Finance and Economics Division.

**Infrastructure and network division (DIR, 8 staff):** designs the methodologies for defining interconnection and infrastructure capacity, the capacity allocation and congestion management mechanisms, the access rules and transparency obligations for network and infrastructure operators and the technical rules for system operation, measurement, reading, processing and provision of energy data. In addition, it monitors the efficiency and the technical quality of service of regulated networks and infrastructures. It further ensures technical co-ordination between interconnected network operators and their interoperability, network and infrastructure investment projects and compliance with national and European network development plans. The division will be maintained in the new structure.

**Markets and consumers division (DMC, 12 staff)**: designs supervisory mechanisms and monitors wholesale and retail markets. It also defines criteria and methodologies applicable to switching and energy labeling. It analyzes the level of competition in the wholesale and retail energy markets, the performance of agents and liberalisation processes, the evolution of the renewables sectors and green certificate markets. The division also monitors the application of regulatory provisions on switching and the evolution of supply and demand structure. In the new structure, the division will focus on markets and competition (as a renamed Markets and Competition Division), while the consumer issues will be absorbed into the new Energy Consumers Division.

**Pricing and tariffs division (DTP, 10 staff):** defines methodologies and models for the pricing of regulated activities, the price of connections and services provided by networks and infrastructures, the marginal and incremental costs, the definition of tariff structures and options, the billing variables and their rules. The division is also in charge of the regulatory incentives to promote energy efficiency. It analyses regulatory mechanisms and models for forecasting tariff and price developments and monitors prices by applying the principle of tariff additivity and the timeliness of regulated tariffs. The division will be renamed as Tariffs, Pricing and Energy Efficiency Division under the new structure.

**General administration division (DAG, 20 staff):** in charge of human resource management, financial management, logistics and procurement, IT systems management and document management. DAG is responsible for ensuring the execution of management and organisational actions in the mentioned areas, as well as promoting the application of norms and procedures of technical, administrative and technological modernisation. It will be maintained in the new structure.

**Legal division (DSJ, 7 staff):** The legal division ensures legal support for the elaboration of regulations, administrative activities and internal procedures. It also is responsible for certification, compliance, sanctioning and enforcement activities of ERSE. It ensures the representation of ERSE in court proceedings. It will be maintained in the new structure.

**National Petroleum System Installation Commission (CISPN, 4 staff):** an internal "founding committee" for the National Petroleum System, to implement ERSE's new responsibilities regarding fuels and biofuels. This is the only sector-specific team in ERSE. In the re-organisation, the work performed by this Commission may be integrated into another division, or the team may continue as a sector-specific unit, given that the fuels sector has specificities that distinguish it from the electricity and natural gas sectors. Furthermore, the fuels sector does not have a European legislative framework that supports regulatory activity.

*New teams to be created through the process of restructuring*

**The Innovation and Special Projects Development Office (IDEP)** will be responsible for contributing to the active representation of ERSE in entities, associations, conferences, forums, projects and think tanks, consolidating internal teams by strengthening training for innovation, encouraging national debate around the themes of energy and innovation in the regulated sectors, enhancing academic knowledge on energy regulation and bringing in new participants to the debate on the future of energy.

**The Directorate-General for Regulation (DGR)** will co-ordinate the preparation of strategic plans and reports, carry out cross-cutting activities, continuously analyse the effectiveness of regulation, monitor the statistical and aggregate treatment of regulatory information and advise the Board of Directors and institutional representation of ERSE.

**The Internal Management Office (GGI)** will be tasked with conceiving and implementing an internal system of control to promote a culture of compliance and risk-management involving all staff and accompanying the execution of strategic plans and reports, and cross-cutting issues.

**The International Relations Office** (**GRI**) (currently part of the Support to the Board unit) will be responsible for co-ordinating European and international activities, as well as providing technical support to the Board of Directors and ERSE services, in terms of strategic positions, European and international decisions, meetings and activities.

**A Data Protection Officer** will ensure compliance with the General Data Protection Regime (**GDPR**).

The work of the current Markets and Consumers Division will be split, to consolidate all work concerning energy consumers in one division (the Energy Consumers Division) and market monitoring activities in another division, the Markets and Competition Division. The **Energy Consumers Division (DCE)** will be responsible for designing indicators of commercial service quality, satisfaction assessment surveys and information or training actions for energy consumers; analysing the contracts proposed by suppliers to customers, complaints and requests for information from energy consumers, legislative and regulatory protection measures and the instruments necessary for an effective safeguarding of the rights and interests of energy consumers; monitoring compliance with commercial service quality indicators and technical support for handling complaints and requests for information from energy consumers. The current ACE will be placed within this division. The **Markets and Competition Division (DMC)** will be responsible for designing supervisory mechanisms and monitoring the wholesale, retail, $CO_2$ emission license and green certificate markets, defining criteria and methodologies applicable to switching suppliers and energy labelling; analysing the level of competition in the wholesale and retail energy markets, the performance of agents and the liberalisation processes, the evolution of the renewables sectors and the green certificate markets; monitoring the application of regulatory provisions on switching suppliers and the evolution of the supply and demand structure.

## *Regulatory quality tools*

### *Ex ante assessments*

No formal *ex ante* assessment is mandatory for ERSE activities, except in some areas where they are required under European regulation. Although ERSE does not undertake systematic *ex ante* assessment of costs and benefits, every ERSE decision must be subject to formal hearings (either public or for the stakeholders affected by the decision) and must be accompanied by a justification document. The justification document may include scenario analysis, impact evaluation, explanation of the regulation's intention, its legal framework, etc. All *ex ante* analyses are publically available.

There is no explicit proportionality requirement that requires ERSE to tailor the level of the assessment to the potential impacts of a new regulation. Nevertheless, the level of detail used in the ex-ante analysis depends on the type of decision and its general impacts. If it is a decision on tariffs and regulated companies' revenues (either on methodologies or on parameters), the economic analysis is detailed and data on costs and benefits are usually included. If the decision is about operational procedures, the analysis usually focuses more on technical requirements, service output performance and customer interaction (simplicity, easy access, time frames, etc.).

Cost-benefit analyses are performed depending on the legal framework or internal processes that apply. Currently, each head of division is responsible for determining whether a CBA is needed and for co-ordinating the analysis. The assessment is then submitted to the Board for consideration before a regulatory decision is taken. A new division (GGI) is currently being established in the context of ERSE's restructuring that will review and develop internal processes and quality control procedures, including for CBAs. Examples of activities where ERSE performs CBAs are:

- Introduction of new tariff structures
- *Ex ante* analyses of regulatory methodologies in regulatory reviews and parameter setting that focus on the impact on allowed revenues for regulated activities
- In the context of the network development and investment plans for natural gas, ERSE analyses the geographic coverage of natural gas networks using qualitative (e.g. universal access to natural gas) and quantitative criteria (e.g. economic rationality of expansion for municipalities not served by the networks)
- In the context of the National Petroleum System, ERSE has been mandated by the government and by the parliament to perform CBA studies on relevant projects, namely the pipelines for connecting the Sines Maritime Terminal of Liquid Bulks to the multiproduct pipeline between Sines and Aveiras de Cima, a storage facility for fuels and LPG in Sines, and the jet pipeline between Aveiras de Cima and the Lisbon Airport.

In general, the benefits assessed in the CBAs amount to the costs avoided for the regulated sectors. The methodology does not tend to assess other types of costs and benefits, such as societal, environmental, etc. The types of costs include:

- the impact on the system costs and income to be recovered by tariffs
- the profitability of regulated activities
- the stability of the level of revenues.

ERSE's consultative councils have confirmed the public accessibility and clarity of ex ante assessments, including CBAs. They receive them together with relevant documentation whenever they are consulted on a proposed decision.

ERSE also analyses CBAs that are done by other actors. For example, ERSE analyses the methodology and the results of the CBAs that regulated companies include in their investment plans.

#### Ex post *reviews*

ERSE does not have a standard methodology for *ex post* reviews but most activities feature them. There are two cycles of *ex post* reviews:

- Once a year, *ex post* reviews are performed within the tariff setting process.
- In addition, *ex post* reviews take place every three to four years, whenever a regulatory period comes to an end. It enables ERSE to assess how the regulatory parameters and incentives have worked (vis-à-vis the market actors' performance) and where changes might be needed for the subsequent period.[13]

Beside these cycles of *ex post* reviews, there is also the possibility of performing these evaluations on an *ad hoc* basis whenever necessary. The evaluations are co-ordinated by the respective heads of division, who then submit them to the Board.

The main quantitative criteria taken into account are the impact on system costs and revenues to be recovered from tariffs, the profitability of regulated activities and the stability of the level of revenues, as is the case in the context of *ex ante* evaluations. In the review process of regulatory methodologies, *ex post* and *ex ante* evaluations are interdependent. In general, the criteria are published by ERSE in its codes/regulations and supporting documents.

### *Inspections, audits and enforcement*

#### *Inspections and audits*

ERSE carries out inspections and audits as part of its supervisory duties, and to date has focused exclusively on the electricity and gas sectors. Audits are generally undertaken on the regulated companies (i.e. network operators and the Logistics Operator for Switching Suppliers, OLMC), while inspections are also applied for other energy actors, such as electricity and gas suppliers. However, audits and inspections are possible across all market actors (regulated or not). Regarding the fuels sector, the legal framework foresees the possibility for ERSE to do audits, but given the shared competence with ENSE and ENSE's key function in this regard, ERSE is not planning any audits or inspections. Any potential for jurisdictional overlap, for example, with enforcement work by ENSE for the fuels sector or consumer protection by ASAE, is managed via Memoranda of Understanding (MoUs). At working level, ERSE has access to information on past and planned ENSE audits. Audits and inspections are also within ERSE remit for electric mobility,[14] but in this early stage of the sector's development, none have been envisaged so far.

ERSE divisions verify the compliance of regulated entities through inspections and audits according to their area of responsibility. If a division discovers any fact or suspicion of wrongdoing by a market agent or operator in the course of its supervisory activities, this information is sent to the Board, which in turn reports it to the legal affairs division.

The ERSE website lists the inspections and audits that have taken place in the electricity and natural gas sectors. The website makes available the reports on the outcomes of some but not all audits (ERSE, 2020[3]); it does not publish data or information on the outcomes of inspections.

### Inspections

ERSE inspects the entities subject to its regulation and supervision, namely network operators, other regulated infrastructures and energy traders (ERSE, 2020[3]). The Framework Law of Independent Administrative Entities establishes that regulatory bodies shall carry out inspections and audits on an *ad hoc* basis, in execution of previously approved inspection plans and/or whenever there are circumstances that indicate disturbances in the respective sector of activity. For example, an inspection may be triggered in order to investigate complaints that have been submitted. In the past, ERSE has had inspection plans but more recently has carried out inspections on a needs-based approach, based on the data analysis and monitoring of the regulated companies. The regulator can also decide to take action as a result of consumer complaints, if it is concerned that a company practice may be suspicious. Inspections are unannounced. ERSE carried out eight inspections between 2015 and 2019 (Table 2.9).

## Table 2.9. Inspections 2015-19

| Sector | Year | Object of inspection | Company |
|---|---|---|---|
| Gas | 2019 | Conversion and reconversion procedures | REN Portgás Distribuição, S.A. |
| Electricity | 2018 | Billing of special regime producers | EDP Serviço Universal, S.A. |
| Electricity and gas | 2018 | Process to transfer costs and assets to logistics operator for switching suppliers | EDP Distribuição – Energia, S.A. and REN Gasodutos, S.A. |
| Electricity | 2018 | Acquisitions and disposals of real estate associated with the concession for high and medium voltage (electricity) | EDP Distribuição – Energia, S.A. |
| Electricity | 2018 | Process for billing suppliers (electricity) | EDP Distribuição – Energia, S.A. |
| Gas | 2016 | Procedures for buying and selling natural gas | Tagusgás – Empresa de Gás do Vale do Tejo, S.A |

Source:ERSE, Enforcement, https://www.erse.pt/en/activities/enforcement/.

Inspections are carried out by ERSE's regulatory divisions. The framework law lays out the rights and duties of employees mandated when they are carrying out an inspection or audit (article 42). ERSE's legal division (the department with sanctioning powers) does not participate directly in the inspections.

The goal of inspections is to:

- Ensure compliance with the legal and regulatory provisions that are applicable to operators
- Ensure compliance with ERSE instructions and decisions
- Ensure the recovery of regulated tariffs
- Verify compliance by regulated sector agents with public service obligations
- Verify compliance with quality of service standards
- Act on a request of consumer complaints

Legislation does not require inspection and enforcement activities to be risk-based. In practice, ERSE inspection activities may result from:

- The existence of a potential risk that the procedures defined by ERSE or other entities applicable to the case in question are not being followed
- Overseeing the application of the rules and standards established by ERSE in its Tariffs Regulation
- The need to ensure verification of the operating conditions of the national electricity and gas systems
- The need to verify the degree or level of credibility or confidence regarding the compliance and reliability reported by the regulated entities

To fulfil its inspection role, ERSE has the duty and power to:

- Identify the entities infringing the laws and regulations which ERSE is tasked with supervising
- Obtain assistance of administrative or law-enforcement authorities when deemed necessary
- Access the facilities, property, means of transportation and services of the regulated entities, and entities which co-operate with regulated entities, as well as access their documents, books, registries and information and communication systems
- Obtain, by any means, copies of the documents mentioned above
- Require that any legal representative, worker or staff of the regulated entities, answer questions pertaining to facts or documents related to the object and objective of the inspection, as well as registering their responses

**Audits**

ERSE makes use of two categories of audits: one-off or specialised audits after identifying potential situations of non-compliance and regular audits, generally on an annual basis, to certify or verify the information reporting and procedures compliance or to ensure that the records are accurate. In the case of entities that are regulated under the Tariff Regulation, ERSE approves an auditing and oversight plan containing the issues subject to periodic auditing. The plan does not include a calendar of planned audits. ERSE notifies regulated companies by letter well in advance that an audit is due to take place. ERSE carried out 13 audits between 2015 and 2019 (Table 2.10).

## Table 2.10. Audits, 2015-19

| Sector | Year | Object | Company |
|---|---|---|---|
| Electricity | 2019 | Investments at standard costs for 2018 | REN – Rede Eléctrica Nacional, S.A. |
| Gas | 2018 | Information provided during supplier switching process | EDP Gás Distribuição, S.A. and REN Portgás Distribuição, S.A. |
| Electricity | 2018 | Investments at reference costs for 2017 | REN – Rede Eléctrica Nacional, S.A. |
| Electricity | 2018 | Quality of service | EDP Distribuição- Energia, S.A. |
| Gas | 2017 | Procedures for buying and selling natural gas | Tagusgás – Empresa de Gás do Vale do Tejo, S.A. |
| Electricity | 2017 | Investments at reference costs for 2016 | REN – Rede Eléctrica Nacional, S.A. |
| Electricity | 2016 | Investments at reference costs for 2015 | REN – Rede Eléctrica Nacional, S.A. |
| Electricity | 2016 | Monitoring relations between the regulated and non-regulated companies of the group | Grupo REN |
| Electricity | 2016 | Monitoring relations between the regulated and non-regulated companies of the group | Grupo EDP |
| Electricity | 2016 | Quality of service | REN – Rede Eléctrica Nacional, S.A. |
| Electricity | 2015 | Quality of service | EEM – Empresa de Eletricidade da Madeira, S.A. |
| Electricity | 2015 | Quality of service | EDA- Eletricidade dos Açores, S.A. |
| Electricity | 2015 | Investments at reference costs for 2014 | REN – Rede Eléctrica Nacional, S.A. |
| Gas | 2015 | Allocation of the social tariff | Galp Power, S.A. |
| Electricity | 2015 | Allocation of the social tariff | EDP Comercial — Comercialização de Energia, S.A. |

Source: ERSE, Enforcement, https://www.erse.pt/en/activities/enforcement/.

Audits follow the Portuguese Auditing Standards and Guidelines and are mostly performed by independent audit firms. For specialised audits, where ERSE can appoint the auditor, ERSE approves the content and terms of reference of the audit, and approves the auditor's final report. ERSE may also request the entities subject to the Tariff Regulation to initiate additional audits, complementary to the financial auditing. These requests might come up in the context of the certification of the entities' accounts at the end of each financial period.

### *Enforcement*

ERSE can impose a wide range of sanctions.[15] Available sanctions include warnings, fines, and accessory sanctions (prohibition of the exercise of any activity within the scope of the regulated sectors, banning of the exercise of an administrative or management position in entities intervening in the regulated sectors and publication in a newspaper with national coverage or on ERSE's website). Under specific criteria, and with the agreement of the agent, a case can be closed with a procedural transaction.[16]

The different legal frameworks that underpin ERSE's sanctioning powers lead to different enforcement outcomes. Under the Energy Sector Sanctions Framework, the gradation of available sanctions is considered adequate to allow credible deterrence through the escalation of sanctions, given that:

- Setting the amount of the fine can take into account relevant circumstances, including the duration and the consequences of the infringement, the benefits derived from the infringement, the financial situation of the offender, etc.
- The legal framework sets the upper limit of the fine at 2%, 5% and 10% of total turnover depending on the seriousness of the administrative offence, when the infringer is a legal person, and at 5%, 20% and 30% of total annual remuneration earned in the exercise of professional functions, when the infringer is a natural person.
- The maximum applicable fine is double for repeat offenders.

The Energy Sector Sanctions Framework applies to the electricity and natural gas sectors but does not cover fuels, electric mobility or the REMIT Regulation. Other laws beyond the Energy Sector Sanctions Framework, notably other special penalty regimes, confer fragmented sanctioning powers to ERSE in respect to the other sectors. The sanctions provided under the special penalty regimes[17] (e.g. the complaints book and the unfair commercial practices legislation) may not be adequate to allow credible deterrence. For a violation of the complaints book rules,[18] fines are set at a minimum of EUR 150 and a maximum of EUR 15 000 for each infringement depending on the offence, the offender (natural or legal person) and the level of guilt. Regarding unfair commercial practices,[19] fines are set at a minimum of EUR 250 and a maximum of EUR 44 891.81 for each infringement, depending on the offence, the offender (natural or legal person) and the level of guilt. Several cases of repeat offenders indicate that the sanctions under these special penalty regimes are not a credible deterrent.

After the initiation of proceedings, all procedures are public and searchable on request.

## *Consumer protection*

In the context of its consumer protection responsibilities, ERSE has a specific service for informing and supporting energy consumers. It publishes useful information for consumers in a dedicated area on its website, disseminates "Bad Practice Alerts" highlighting unfair commercial practices carried out by energy suppliers, and responds to individual requests for information. In addition to publishing information on its website, ERSE's consumer engagement efforts include publication of short videos, brochures and flyers, public service messages on the radio and television appearances to explain energy issues. ERSE also hosts and manages three online comparison tools for consumers (for example, to compare prices of providers or to know the energy mix and $CO_2$ emissions of their energy consumption).

ERSE provides telephone assistance through a dedicated consumer line, available every working day from 3:00 p.m. to 6:00 p.m, and a face-to-face service, by prior appointment. This specific service for consumers is also responsible for organising and promoting an annual training programme, aimed mainly at consumer associations and arbitration centres for consumer disputes, and participates in events organised by other entities.

ERSE also handles consumer complaints. In 2019, ERSE received 21 358 complaints and requests for information (32% less than in the previous year, 31 421 requests). The sector with the most complaints is electricity. 6 056 complaints or requests related to billing and 2 575 related to energy contracts. ERSE is one of several organisations to whom consumers can direct their complaints in the energy sector. Others include DECO (a private consumer rights organisation), the Directorate-General for Consumer Affairs, arbitration centres, ENSE and ASAE.

Complaints can reach ERSE through several avenues:

- consumers can contact ERSE directly via phone, email or its website;
- complaints from the complaints book that have not been dealt with in time by operators are directed to ERSE automatically; or
- third parties that may have received the complaint in error can redirect it to ERSE (e.g. ENSE, which only deals with complaints in the fuels sector, not the electricity or gas sectors).

Through its Support to Energy Consumers (ACE) team, ERSE tries to resolve complaints and mediate between operators and consumers. After analysing the complaint, ERSE can collect additional elements from consumers or market agents. Unlike other organisations that may receive consumer complaints such as DECO, suppliers/operators are obliged to respond to ERSE's requests for information. For comparison, DECO receives about half the number of complaints or information requests on the energy sector compared to ERSE (11 056 in 2019 and 16 981 in 2018; the main issues concerned billing; contracts and switching suppliers; and unfair commercial practices, including misleading or aggressive sales).[20]

In cases where ACE cannot resolve the complaint and mediation fails, ERSE recommends the use of arbitration as an Alternative Dispute Resolution (ADR) mechanism. If the consumer is an individual person (domestic user) and they decide to submit the dispute to arbitration, the market agent is obliged to accept the arbitration decision. As a characteristic of the Portuguese system, arbitration centres are multi-disciplinary and cover a suite of economic sectors, thus not all are not specialised on energy legislation and regulation. In addition, there are limits on the type of consumers who can access ADR mechanisms (only individual household consumers are covered), as well as an upper monetary amount which can be disputed (EUR 5 000). Users not covered by these characteristics can seek redress against a market agent though the court system.

Recently, ERSE signed co-operation agreements with seven out of the nine arbitration centres for consumer disputes. Within the scope of each protocol, ERSE provides technical and financial support to the arbitration centre, including training. The exceptions are *Centro de Arbitragem da Universidade Autónoma de Lisboa* that functions within a private university and is privately funded and *Centro de Arbitragem de Conflitos de Consumo da Região Autónoma da Madeira*, established by regional authorities. Although they are authorised and recognised by the government, they are not integrated into the national network of arbitration centres.

In cases where a serious infringement is suspected, it is referred to ERSE's legal division for possible enforcement action. Complainants can also file reports of suspected infringement on ERSE's website that are transmitted directly to the legal division. ERSE analyses complaints according to the applicable sanctioning framework. Following this, it can open administrative infraction proceedings, after which ERSE carries out the necessary investigation in order to sanction the natural or legal person or close the case.

According to the Energy Sector Sanctions Framework, if there are not sufficient grounds to follow up on a complaint, ERSE must inform the complainant of the reasons for this assessment. At this point, the complainant can submit their observations in writing within a given timeframe. After receiving these observations, ERSE can open an administrative infraction proceeding or declare the complaint to be unfounded or not a priority for treatment.

## *Engagement and transparency of engagement process*

### *Consultative councils*

ERSE consults key stakeholders on its various decisions through three independent advisory bodies that deliver non-binding opinions: the Advisory Council, the Tariff Council and, since 2019, the Fuels Council.

The councils are collegiate bodies, composed of members defined under the law. They are composed of industry, consumer representatives, representatives from other regulatory entities or public bodies and, in the case of the Advisory Council, government representatives from both national and regional level. Industry and consumer representatives must be represented in equal numbers. Members serve a renewable term of three years; many members have been on the councils for several terms. They are not remunerated for their participation. However, in order to facilitate the participation of household consumer representatives, ERSE allocates a per diem to these members. Each council is chaired by a president, a person of recognised standing and independence appointed by the member of the government responsible for energy. No representatives from ERSE sit on any of the councils, although councils may request that ERSE staff attend meetings to present and explain the proposed decisions under discussion. The President of the Board of ERSE also interacts regularly and directly with the presidents of each council.

Each council sets its own rules of procedure and decides how often to meet. In general, the councils meet several times per month and sometimes, several times a week. Meetings are held at ERSE's premises. Members who are not based in Lisbon are expected to travel to all meetings. The councils may meet extraordinarily if convened at the initiative of the president or at the initiative of at least two-thirds of its members (Advisory Council) or of at least one third of its members (Tariff and Fuels Councils). All opinions of the councils are approved by majority vote, although if members do not agree with all or parts of the opinion of the council they can state this in the submission to ERSE.

The opinions of the councils are made public and published on the ERSE website (ERSE, 2020[4]). If the opinions of the councils do not lead to a change in ERSE's proposed decision, the regulator must justify why it is not making the suggested changes.

ERSE has provided training on energy regulation and related subjects to consumer representatives that sit on the councils in order to build their capacity (which tends to be weaker than that of industry representatives) and thereby enable more meaningful input to council deliberations.

#### Advisory Council

The Advisory Council can meet in plenary or in specific groups pertaining to different sectors: electricity and natural gas. In addition to its president, the council brings together 54 representatives from a wide range of interests, including from government, the environment agency, local and regional governments, regulators, regulated industry, consumer associations, automobile and non-electrified road transport interests, agricultural interests, and LPG-consuming economic activities interests (see Annex 2.A for more information on the composition of the Advisory Council).

The Advisory Council provides a forum for consultation on the definition of ERSE's broad lines of action and deliberations taken by the Board of Directors. In its plenary sessions, it issues opinions on:

- ERSE activity plan and budget
- ERSE annual reports and accounts
- The tariff regulations, whose proposals to this effect are submitted to it by the Board of Directors.[21]
- Other matters common to the electricity and natural gas sectors, including those of a regulatory

nature that are submitted by the Board of Directors, excluding those within the remit of the Tariff Council.

The Advisory Council meeting in sections can issue an opinion on the following:

- Proposals concerning the approval or amendment of regulations that ERSE is responsible for issuing, relating to the electricity and natural gas sectors, with the exception of tariff regulations.
- Proposals relating to opinions that ERSE is responsible for issuing and which the Board of Directors submits for its analysis.
- Other matters related to the electricity sector or with the natural gas sector submitted by the Board of Directors for its analysis, except those matters under the jurisdiction of the Tariff Council.

**Tariff Council**

The Tariff Council provides a specific forum for consultation on tasks assigned to ERSE in the scope of tariffs and prices. The Tariff Council delivers opinions on the approval and review of tariff regulations, as well as on the establishment of tariffs and prices. As with the other councils, industry and consumer representatives must be represented in equal numbers (See Annex 2.B for more information on the constitution of the Tariff Council).

**Fuels Council**

ERSE consults with the Fuels Council within the scope of its duties for the sectors of liquefied petroleum gas (LPG) in all its categories, namely bottled, piped or bulk LPG, as well as of petroleum-derived fuels and biofuels. (See Annex 2.C for more information on the composition of the Fuels Council). The council has two sections representing different sectors: i) oil-based fuels and biofuels, and ii) liquefied petroleum gas. Each section decides upon the following matters:

- Proposals for agreement or amendment of the regulations issued by ERSE
- Proposals for opinions within ERSE's competence and that the Board of Directors intend to submit to it.

There is no consultative council for the electric mobility sector. ERSE faced the challenge of identifying relevant stakeholders to consult when it launched a public consultation pertaining to this sector. Some issues relating to electric mobility were however discussed in the Tariff and Advisory councils. Furthermore, the Infrastructure and Networks Division has established informal stakeholder groups with which to interact on this subject. The division meets with all the interested stakeholders that contact ERSE about this topic and aims to disseminate information to the target consumers. As a relatively new sector within ERSE, there was not standardised approach, but some stakeholders were already members of ERSE's councils while others were identified by responding to public consultations.

### *Public consultations*

According to its statutes, and in addition to the work of the councils, all decisions on codes and regulations must be preceded by a public consultation. A mandatory consultation process applies to all its regulatory decisions across all the sectors within its purview. Decisions must be put to public consultation for at least 30 working days or, for urgent cases and sub-regulations, at least 8 consecutive days (although this express process is rarely used). During this period, the councils are also consulted. ERSE conducted 13 public consultations in 2019 and seven in 2018 (Box 2.2).[22]

**Box 2.2. ERSE public consultations, 2018 and 2019**

In 2019, ERSE held 13 public consultations:

- Smart Electricity Grids
- Regulatory Review of Natural Gas
- Parameters for the conditions for connection to the electricity grid
- Directive that establishes the regulatory framework for the mechanism for contracting electricity in order to satisfy the consumption of customers of the supplier of last resort
- Five-year Network Development Plan for electricity distribution
- Designation and characteristics of the members of the Advisory Council, the Fuels Council and the Tariff Council
- Process for storage, collection and exchange of Liquefied Petroleum Gas (LPG) bottles
- Pre-consultation on the rules of the Energy Efficiency Promotion Plan
- Electric Mobility Regulation
- Regulation on the fulfilment of consumer information obligations by petroleum-based fuels and liquefied petroleum gas (LPG) traders
- Risk and Guarantee Management scheme for the national electricity system
- Self-consumption
- Merging the Electricity and Natural Gas Commercial Relations Regulations

In 2018, ERSE held seven public consultations:

- Review of the gas Tariff Regulation and Commercial Relations Regulation
- Ten Year Network Development Plan for electricity transmission
- Proposals on the terms and conditions of the new concession contracts for low voltage electricity distribution
- Implementation of the EU Gas Transmission Tariff Network Code
- Rules for the pilot project on demand participation in the electricity balancing market
- Review of the electricity Tariff Regulation
- Five Year Network Development Plan for gas distribution

Source: (ERSE, 2020[5]), Concluídas, https://www.erse.pt/atividade/consultas-publicas/concluidas/.

ERSE must notify the member of the government responsible for energy, DGEG and all stakeholders of the regulated sectors registered for consultation, including concession holders, licensees, traders and consumer associations, and provide them with access to the relevant documents through the ERSE website. Registration for public consultations can be made using forms provided on the ERSE website. All stakeholders registered for public consultations receive the documents at the same time as they are published on the ERSE website (ERSE, 2020[4]).

Data and information provided to stakeholders during the consultation process, include:

- The draft regulation and supporting documents justifying the proposals. Sometimes this can include impact assessments and/or a discussion of alternative options
- Q&As and supporting documents written in plain language when the audience is non expert
- For tariff decisions, all assumptions and regulatory data supporting the proposal

All comments received during the public consultation are published unless the respondent requests confidentiality. ERSE then prepares a document where it addresses all the topics raised in the consultation and justifies why the proposed changes were or were not accepted.

For tariff decisions specifically – i.e. applying the current tariff regulation and determining the prices for tariffs and the allowed revenues of the operators – ERSE issues a proposal for the prices and all the supporting information to the Tariff Council and to the regulated companies only. This proposal is confidential. Within one month, the Tariff Council gives its formal opinion. ERSE then considers that opinion and takes the final tariff decision which is made public via the ERSE website and in Portugal's Official Bulletin.

For particularly complex or sensitive issues, ERSE may conduct pre-consultations with stakeholders through the same public consultation platform. The purpose is to ensure open discussions on topics before the presentation of the regulation proposal, in order to identify and understand the main concerns of the stakeholders and potentially guide the drafting of the regulation proposal. This process is then followed by a regular consultation process.

For the majority of its regulatory reviews, ERSE organises a public hearing for stakeholders, during the consultation period, in order to promote a more dynamic and interactive discussion on the proposals. For example, ERSE presented its project to merge the Electricity and Natural Gas Industry Relations Regulations; more than 180 participants registered.

Additionally, ERSE can hold meetings with stakeholders to hear from specific perspectives outside the broader public consultation process. ERSE does not publish a list of these meetings or their minutes.

Separately, ERSE may have meetings with formal "support groups" composed of stakeholders, for which the documentation and minutes is kept for legal and administrative purposes. This information is not published, but can be accessed upon request (e.g. freedom of information provisions and right of recourse of administrative procedures).

### Box 2.3. Ensuring transparency at ERSE

The following legislative requirements are in place to enhance the transparency of ERSE's activities (with confidential and commercially sensitive information appropriately removed if needed):

- Public consultation on relevant activities
- Publication of all decisions, resolutions and agreements
- Publication of all comments received during the public consultation (unless the respondent requires confidentiality) and of a document where it addresses all the topics raised in the consultation and justifies why the proposed changes were or were not accepted
- The formal opinions of the councils are also made public. When their opinion is not followed, ERSE must justify why
- Publication of a forward-looking action plan

Mechanisms to reach out to stakeholders and explain the rationale for its decisions once the decisions have been taken include:

- Use of the website to communicate and explain decisions
- For issues with big impact in society, ERSE has organised workshops and training sessions across the country. For example, regarding the annual tariffs decision ERSE usually holds a session open to all consumers and consumer associations for explain the changes in the electricity and gas prices.

Source: ERSE, 2020.

## Appeals

The decisions taken by ERSE within the scope of its sanctioning powers (see *Enforcement*) may be appealed to the Competition, Regulation and Supervision Court within a period of 20 or 30 working days.

- The appeal must be submitted to ERSE, with allegations and conclusions.
- ERSE must send the case file to the Public Prosecutor's Office with all the relevant elements and evidence.
- If relevant, the Public Prosecutor's Office may forward the case to the judge or drop the indictment, after hearing ERSE.
- The court may decide to hold a trial hearing or reach a verdict immediately, in which case ERSE, the Public Prosecutor's Office and the stakeholder may oppose the waiver of the hearing.
- The court shall issue a decision to close the case, acquit or sanction the person and then inform ERSE.
- The decisions of the Competition, Regulation and Supervision Court may be appealed to the competent Court of Appeal, which will decide at the last resort, without prejudice to the jurisdiction of the Portuguese Constitutional Court.

In addition, regulations or administrative acts issued by ERSE (e.g. the annual decision regarding tariffs) may also be appealed before the competent Administrative Court at any time, in case of null acts, or within a period of three months, in case of voidable acts.

- The initial application must be sent directly to the competent court.
- ERSE is summoned to challenge and the Public Prosecutor's Office is notified to pronounce.
- The court may decide immediately or order a pre-trial hearing, for the purpose of attempting to conciliate or define the subsequent terms of the process. If the attempt at conciliation unsuccessful, the court determines to hold a trial hearing, where the evidence is presented.
- The court can acquit or convict, and must inform the parties and the Public Prosecutor's Office.

ERSE must publish the results of all legal appeals.

### Table 2.11. Appeals

| | Number of ERSE decisions taken[1] | Number of ERSE decisions appealed | Status (decision upheld, rejected, on-going) |
|---|---|---|---|
| 2019 | 14 | 0 | n/a |
| 2018 | 25 | 1 | On-going |
| 2017 | 11 | 4 | On-going |
| 2016 | 12 | 2 | On-going |

1 Considers only tariff decisions as well as decisions regarding sanctions. A tariff decision may be appealed by different stakeholders in different parts.
Source: ERSE, 2020.

Moreover, ERSE is subject to the jurisdiction and powers of financial control of the Court of Auditors, namely with regard to the verification of accounts, the supervision of acts and contracts that generate expenses for the entity, the assessment of the legality, economy, effectiveness and efficiency of the entity's financial management, the supervision of its resources and the allocation of financial resources from the European Union, among others.

## Output and outcome

### *Data collection, analysis and management*

ERSE regulations require regulated entities to submit a large amount of data at differing frequencies depending on the type of information (Box 2.4). Each division defines the data reporting requirements for market agents through the regulations and codes that they develop in their respective areas of work, and all regulations and codes are then approved by the Board. Data reporting requirements are generally defined for a regulatory period (three years for the electricity sector and four years for the natural gas sector), which provides some stability and predictability for regulated entities. ERSE has the right nevertheless to request additional information whenever it deems necessary.

Each division requests data from regulated entities based on the requirements in the approved regulations and codes. Some tools are in place to co-ordinate the different data requests. For example, divisions have access to a shared email account from which the data requests are sent to regulated entities. This system avoids regulated entities receiving messages from several different contact points within ERSE. Divisions also rely on informal communications between staff to keep informed about what data is being requested from which companies.

#### Box 2.4. Data reporting requirements for regulated entities

ERSE regulations require all regulated operators to report annually on regulated accounts, which includes information on expenditure, income, assets, liabilities and equity and all other economic and physical information necessary for the regulatory process. The nature and level of the breakdown of economic, financial and operational information is defined for each sector. In particular, the tariff code requires a deep and systematised accounting breakdown of regulated activities. Thus, companies are required to report highly disaggregated data regarding the different nature of expenses, income, assets and liabilities.

ERSE regulations also require regulated entities to submit the following data periodically:

- In the context of commercial quality of service, on a quarterly basis: waiting time in customer centres, phone call waiting time, responses to customer requests and complaints, frequency of meter reading, time of response to emergency situations, scheduling availability for activation/deactivation of supply, reconnection timing after failure, etc.
- In the context of energy measurement, every six months: number of meters installed, verification of meters, meter reading, process of making consumption data available to suppliers, etc.
- In the context of the offers on the retail market to domestic consumers, every six months: loyalty and penalty clauses, means of payment, additional services and price indexation.
- In the context of wholesale market monitoring, on a daily basis: information on day-ahead, intraday and system operation markets from the electricity market operator and from the electricity TSO.
- In the context of supplier switching, the Logistics Operator for Switching Suppliers (OLMC) provides, on a monthly basis: the number of clients (and consumption) that changed supplier, the number of clients and consumption per supplier, number of new contracts per supplier, etc.
- In the context of supplier of last resort acquisitions of renewable and CHP electricity benefiting from feed-in-tariffs, the supplier of last resort sends to ERSE, every month: the energy amounts, prices value of acquisitions, disaggregated by technology.

- In the context of electricity labelling, suppliers must send to ERSE every three months: the total number of clients and associated consumption, the total number of clients and associated consumption disaggregated by commercial offer, acquisition and cancelling of guarantees of origin and bilateral contracts as well as information necessary to calculate the national energy mix.
- In the context of electricity connections, the TSOs and DSOs shall send every year, with a disaggregation by semester of number and capacity of new connections, number of requests to increase capacity, amounts in EUR supported by the client requesting the connection.
- For the process of the storage, collection and exchange of Liquefied Petroleum Gas (LPG) bottles, the operators of the LPG botted storage facilities must report monthly to ERSE the LPG bottles recovered by the companies as well as the remaining stocks and the compulsory withdrawal notices issued by them.
- In the context of the fees applied to gas networks for using public land, every year the DSOs must send the costs borne from these fees, the amounts of the fees transferred to suppliers and the debt to be recovered in the following years (difference between the total costs borne and the total amount transferred to suppliers), disaggregated by municipality. Every year suppliers must send the amounts of these fees transferred to customers, also disaggregated by municipality.

**Invoiced Prices – Electricity and Natural Gas**

Regarding its activity of monitoring the retail energy prices, electricity and gas suppliers, ERSE requires the following information:

- Total consumption (quarter and year): total value of electricity and natural gas consumption for the period of consumption under analysis, for the different time periods.
- Total contracted power (quarter and year): total value of contracted power or capacity for the period of consumption under analysis.
- Number of customers (quarter and year): average number of customers for the consumption period under analysis.
- Average prices (quarter and year): average value invoiced (with and without taxes), for the consumption period under analysis.

**Fuels**

Regarding ERSE's activity of supervising and monitoring the logistics and the retail market of fuels and LPG, the National Petroleum System undertakings should report on the "*Balcão Unico*" platform the following data:

- The daily prices of fuels and LPG on the retail market
- The monthly quantities of fuels and LPG produced by the refineries, handled in the logistic infrastructures and marketed in service stations or commercialised in the LPG sales facilities
- The quantities of petroleum products introduced in the national market, at the wholesale level, for the purposes of tax, strategic reserves and ERSE's contribution.

**Electricity and Natural Gas Offers**

- Prices and commercial conditions for electricity offers (low voltage level) from energy suppliers.
- Prices and commercial conditions for gas offers (low pressure level) from energy suppliers.
- Prices and commercial conditions for dual offers (low voltage and low pressure levels) from energy suppliers.

**Electricity and Natural Gas vulnerable customers**

- Number of electricity vulnerable customers, with social electricity tariffs (quarterly).
- Number of gas vulnerable customers, with social gas tariffs (quarterly).

Source: ERSE, 2020.

Although there is no scheduled periodic review of reporting requirements, in practice ERSE often reviews reporting obligations in terms of their usefulness in order to adapt to changes in the market or regulation (regulatory changes or regulatory period changes). If the need does arise to adjust the reporting requirements, a formal process is launched and new rules are published. For example, the requirements of the information presented in the regulated accounts for calculating allowed revenues are defined by the complementary rules and methodologies as set out in the tariff regulation. In 2019, ERSE revised and published new complementary standards for both the electricity and natural gas sectors.

Currently, there is no central portal for actors to submit data. Given the volume of data required by the regulatory process and, especially, supervision activities, ERSE has been implementing a strategy for using and structuring data using business intelligence tools and IT systems (Box 2.5). ERSE tends to rely on specialised external service providers in combination with its internal technical support teams and the regulatory teams to develop these systems. In autumn 2019, ERSE launched an internal working group to review and map the various data and communication tools used by the divisions, with a view to developing a strategy for their efficiency, interoperability and modernisation. In addition, ERSE is investing in IT systems that will enable the establishment of more complete databases that can support new uses and data processing. In addition, several projects are underway to make various data collection obligations "smarter" and more automated.

### Box 2.5. Data tools used at ERSE

ERSE uses the Market Information System (SIMER), a market intelligence analysis system to ensure structured data processing and knowledge production with the information gathered through the supervision process.

ERSE uses "power bi" and other tools in order to improve its performance, for example for the online comparison tools.

ERSE uses the "*Balcão Unico*" system, a joint platform shared by ERSE, ENSE, LNEG and DGEG, hosted by ENSE, for supervising and monitoring the petroleum products and biofuels sectors.

ERSE developed, together with an external service provider, a new application to support the calculations of allowed revenues of the activities of electric sector, which includes a structured database to gather and store data, functionalities to deal with the recurrent calculations and a tool to analyse the financial sustainability of the electric sector.

ERSE uses several econometric software programmes, such as E-Views and STATA, to perform econometric analyses (for example, frontier efficiency analysis econometric models, multiple regression models with sectional data and panel data, and Data Envelopment Analysis – DEA).

One of the tools available to energy consumers to submit complaints or requests for information is the Livro de Reclamações Eletrónico (Online Complaints Book), with a direct link to ERSE's complaints management system. ERSE receives a copy of the complaints addressed to the companies and the corresponding response to the consumer, for review and possible intervention. Requests for information are only received and answered by ERSE.

Source: ERSE, 2020.

The main challenges associated with data collection are:

- An increasing number of (non-traditional) players in the energy sector who may not be used to receiving such data requests.[23]
- Obtaining information in the appropriate disaggregation/detail, e.g. segmented by activity or function when they are performed by the same operator, as resources are sometimes common to various activities or functions.
- Certification of the information by an independent entity (audit of accounts and other regulatory data). Regulated sectors have very complex specificities that are not found in most companies. In this sense, certification will only be accurate if the independent entity is aware of these specificities.
- The existence of different accounting options or standards that impact the reporting of economic and financial information.
- Obtaining comparable economic, financial and physical information from regulated operators to allow benchmarking analysis. This exercise is particularly complex when regulated sectors are characterised by natural monopolies.

Generally speaking, ERSE makes public the information it receives and aggregates from regulated entities through structured reports to the general public and in the documents it prepares for public or stakeholder consultation. However, much of the data that ERSE handles is commercially sensitive or confidential and therefore not published.

### *Monitoring and reporting on the performance of the sector*

ERSE monitors specific indicators in order to assess the performance of regulated entities:

- In terms of commercial quality of service: waiting time in customer centres, waiting times on phone calls, answers to customers complaints and requests of information, scheduling availability, meter reading frequency, timely answer to emergency situations and reconnection.
- In terms of technical quality of service: indicators on continuity of supply (frequency and duration of interruptions) and compliance with quality standards, both for gas and electricity.
- In terms of metering and consumption data: meters installation, parametrisation and verification, meter readings (frequency, extraordinary readings, remote readings), consumer data availability delays and fraud detection.

Regarding the direct outcome of regulatory decisions, ERSE's legal division manages the enforcement and fines processes, including the publication of its decisions as well as a summary of the fines that have been issued. This latter list is included in ERSE's annual report. This activity, together with the monitoring of the performance of the markets and of the market agents and periodic inspections/audits of the companies, allows ERSE to assess compliance with and the outcomes of its decisions.

Regarding wider outcomes, ERSE's monitoring efforts focus in particular on the performance of the wholesale and retail markets and on consumer welfare, including through the analysis of the consumer complaints it receives.

ERSE's reporting on the performance of the sectors includes:

- Reports on the industry and market performance of the regulated sector, e.g. Annual quality of service report[24]
- Reports on the economic performance of the regulated sector, e.g. Investment monitoring of gas networks[25]
- Report of the performance evaluation of regulated activities in the natural gas sector and the electricity sector: this report briefly presents the evolution of several economic and financial indicators for assessing the performance of companies or regulated activities and the effectiveness of regulatory methodologies

- Quarterly electronic newsletters on a number of other issues
- An annual report for the European Commission presenting the main developments in the electricity and natural gas markets in Portugal, including competition (both in the wholesale and retail markets), security of supply and consumer protection

### *Monitoring and reporting on the performance of ERSE*

Legislation requires ERSE to publish a report on its activities on a regular basis.[26] The Board prepares an annual report (including annual accounts) which is submitted to the Statutory Auditor and the Advisory Council for their opinions. These documents must be sent to the government and to the parliament, along with the opinion of the Advisory Council, for approval within 60 days.

The annual report is a detailed and comprehensive report (~165 pages) of ERSE's activities that lists, among other things, the regulations and codes issued by ERSE and all the formal opinions published by ERSE in the course of the year. Parts of the report can be fairly technical in nature.

Every year, ERSE's president presents the annual budget to the parliament. The president is also invited on different occasions to present to the parliament. During these hearings, ERSE may be asked about its performance, the development of the market, the impact of policies and other issues.

In addition, ERSE reports annually to the European Commission and the Agency for the Cooperation of Energy Regulators (ACER) on its activities and the developments in the Portuguese electricity and natural gas markets.

Currently, the regulator does not report against a comprehensive set of performance indicators. However, ERSE is defining key performance indicators (KPIs) for the first time in the context of its strategic plan 2019-2022. ERSE is in the process of defining the KPIs for each division, with the expectation that they will be approved in 2020. ERSE is defining its KPIs independently, not in consultation with the government or the parliament.

In order to gain greater insight into consumer satisfaction and perception regarding its activity, ERSE launched a survey in 2019. Preliminary results released in mid-2020 show that ERSE is regarded by the industry as showing impartiality, professionalism, rigour and credibility. The report identified areas for improvement, including: the visibility of ERSE to final consumers (including ERSE's role in the process of resolving disputes between consumers and market operators), the need to anticipate regulation in the context of a rapidly-changing market, and the visibility of sanctions.

## Notes

[1] As amended by Decree-Laws No. 200/2002, of 25 September, 212/2012, of 25 September 84/2013, of 25 June, 57-A/2018, of 13 July and 76/2019, of 3 June.

[2] Mandate extended to the regulation of natural gas by Decree Law nº 97/2002, of 12 April, within the context of the 1998 EU Directive on the natural gas market. See OECD (2010), Better Regulation in Europe: Portugal, http://www.oecd.org/gov/regulatory-policy/44830175.pdf.

[3] Decree-Law No. 212/2012, of 25 September.

[4] The Decree-Law No. 84/2013, of 25 June, completing the transposition of Directives 2009/72/EC and 2009/73/EC, of the European Parliament and of the Council, of 13 July 2009, that establish the common rules for the internal electricity and natural gas market.

[5] Decree-Law No. 57-A/2018, of 13 July.

[6] Articles 9 and 10 of the Decree Law No. 97/2002, of 12 April.

[7] Pilot Project 2020 "use of technical quality of service data from smart meters".

Pilot project 2020 "vehicle to grid in the Azores".

Pilot project 2019 "Participation of the Demand Response in the Portuguese Balancing Market".

Pilot project 2018/2019 on "Dynamic Access Tariffs".

[8] Articles 3, No. 4, al. a) and 16 of ERSE's Statutes.

[9] Articles 15 and 17 of ERSE's Statutes.

[10] Articles 11 No. , al. d) and 13, No. 1, al. e) of ERSE's Statutes.

[11] Article 14 of ERSE Statutes.

[12] Article 19 of ERSE's Statutes. Articles 2 of the Energy Sector Sanctions Framework, Law No. 9/2013, of 28 January. General Regime of Administrative Offences, approved by Decree-Law No. 433/82, of 27 October.

[13] Articles 21, 32 and 35 of Energy Sector Sanctions Framework.

[14] See Decree-Law No. 156/2005, of 15 September, regarding complaint books, and Decree-Law No. 57/2008, of 26 March, that sanctions unfair commercial practices.

[15] Article 15 of ERSE's Statues.

[16] This competence was transferred to ERSE by the amendment of Decree-Law 31/2006 of 15 February set out by Article 7 of the Decree-Law 69/2019 of 27 August.

[17] Leeway for co-operation agreements is enabled through the ERSE's Statutes, on Article 57, No. 2. See https://www.erse.pt/en/institutional/cooperation/.

[18] Article 3 of Law No. 67/2013, of 28 August, which sets the framework law for independent administrative entities with functions to regulate the economic activity of the private, public and cooperative sectors.

[19] See Articles 3, No. 4, al. a), 10, 16, 59 of ERSE Statutes.

Article 59: Co-operation with the Government and *Assembleia da República*

> 1. Without prejudice to its operational and decision-making independence, ERSE shall keep the Government properly informed about its regulatory activity, through the member of the Government responsible for energy, reporting in particular on recommendations, legislative proposals and draft external regulations which ERSE intends to adopt, as well as on instruments in the framework of the Government's general policy for regulated sectors. 2. ERSE shall also be required to provide in a timely manner all information requested by the member of the

Government responsible for energy that is related to the implementation of annual and multiannual activity plans, the budget and respective

[20] This Plan is mandatory for Public Entities and was also adopted by ERSE.

[21] Redes Energéticas Nacionais (REN) is the current concession holder of both the national electricity transmission grid and the national natural gas transportation grid.

[22] Indicators on Governance of Sector Regulators survey 2018.

[23] Pursuant to Ordinance No. 343-A/2019, of 16 May.

[24] ERSE does not have the power to impose fines in the electric mobility sector (see section on sanctioning powers).

[25] Decree-Law No. 156/2005, of 15 September.

[26] Decree-Law No. 57/2008, of 26 March.

[27] General Regime of Administrative Offences, approved by Decree Law nº 433/82, of 27 October.

[28] Article 49-A of ERSE's Statutes.

[29] Article 33, No. 2 of the Framework Law of Independent Administrative Entities states that budget blocks are not applicable to funds whose source is outside the State Budget.

[30] The court decision is available here: www.tcontas.pt/pt-pt/ProdutosTC/acordaos/3s/Documents/2017/ac021-2017-3s.pdf.

[31] Law No. 8/2012, of 21 February.

[32] This provision was set in the 2019 State Budget Law, and has been included on occasion in previous state budgets. The State Budget Law 2020 foresees the same provision.

[33] Standard templates are provided by the Directorate-General for Budget for all public entities and which detail the budget lines that need to be included, such as general expenditure, human resources and so on.

[34] The sole auditor is an independent, external auditor that is appointed by the Ministry of Finance from a list of accredited firms for a four-year period.

[35] Law No. 71/2018 of December 31, which approved the State Budget for 2019, changed article 38.1 of the Framework Law of Independent Administrative Entities which had stated that regulators were exempt from the national accounting rules that apply to public sector bodies.

[1] All personnel numbers as of 31 December 2019.

[2] European Commission (2018), "A comparative overview of public administration characteristics and performance in EU28". Turnover rate based on evidence that was collected by an EC research project between end 2016 and April 2017.
https://ec.europa.eu/social/main.jsp?catId=738&langId=en&pubId=8072

[1] Article 54 of ERSE's Statutes.

[2] Provisions included in the annual State Budget Laws.

[3] Article 131.º, No. 2, of Labour Code.

[4] Article 31.º of ERSE's Statutes .

[5] Article 33.º of ERSE's Statutes.

[6] Article 30º, No. s 1 and 2 of ERSE's Statutes.

[7] However, the law does not specify which independent entity and there is no precedent.

[8] Article 30º, No. s 3 and 4 of the ERSE's Statutes.

[9] Article 30º, No. s 4 and 5 of ERSE's Statutes.

[10] Article 29, No. 2, al. a) of ERSE's Statutes.

[11] The internal procedures for board meetings are currently being updated to reflect *de facto* practice, as the current document pre-dates the existence of the board's digital platform.

[12] This team is currently housed within the Support to the Board of Directors unit.

[13] The latest reports for the gas (2019) and electricity (2017) sectors respectively: https://www.erse.pt/media/vjagvksn/analise-de-desempenho.pdf and https://www.erse.pt/media/rl0p2ppk/an%C3%A1lise-de-desempenho-se.pdf.

[14] In line with Decree-Law 90/2014.

[15] See The Energy Sector Sanctions Framework, approved by Law No. 9/2013, of 28 January.

[16] Articles 14, 15, 19 and 20 of Energy Sector Sanctions Framework.

[17] Decree-Law nº 156/2005, of 15 September, regarding complaint books, and Decree-Law nº 57/2008, of 26 March, that sanctions unfair commercial practices.

[18] Under article 9 of Decree-Law No. 156/2005, of 15 September.

[19] According to article 21 of Decree-Law No. 57/2008, of 26 March.

[20] Information received from DECO, March 2020.

[21] According to article 43º, No. 1, al. c) of ERSE Statues. Article 43.4(c) however also establishes that the Advisory Council can examine other issues – except those under the Tariff Council's remit. In practice, the Advisory Council does not provide an opinion on tariffs, given the specific responsibility of the Tariffs Council in this regard. The interpretation applied is that they could provide an opinion if called upon to do so by the Board of Directors.

[22] ERSE public consultations webpage, https://www.erse.pt/atividade/consultas-publicas/ .

[23] As an example, the first Portuguese auction of solar energy injection capacity held in 2019 included a company related to the poultry production sector, which took one of the lots. This situation adds to the challenge of obtaining detailed and disaggregated information with an adequate level of reliability about the activity carried out by operators. This challenge increases in the case of information from market operators who, in certain cases, are not required to make this information available or are not subject to the sanctioning power of ERSE. And even in the case of making information available, it does not respect the requirements defined for the companies or regulated entities.

[24] Electricity quality of service assessment, https://www.erse.pt/eletricidade/qualidade-de-servico/ .

[25] Natural gas quality of service assessment, https://www.erse.pt/gas-natural/qualidade-de-servico/ .

[26] Article 7-A of ERSE's Statutes.

## References

ERSE (2020), *Concluídas*, https://www.erse.pt/atividade/consultas-publicas/concluidas/ (accessed on 16 December 2020). [5]

ERSE (2020), *Enforcement*, https://www.erse.pt/en/activities/enforcement/ (accessed on 16 December 2020). [3]

ERSE (2020), *Parecer sobre "Regulamentação do Regime de Autoconsumo" 82a Consulta Pública*, https://www.erse.pt/media/vxske2ez/cp82_parecerconselhoconsultivo.pdf. [4]

ERSE (2019), *Plano Estratégico e Financeiro Plurianual 2019-2022*, https://www.erse.pt/media/x23cbptt/plano-estrat%C3%A9gico-e-financeiro-plurianual-2019-2022.pdf. [1]

ERSE (2019), *Protocols*, https://www.erse.pt/en/institutional/cooperation/ (accessed on 16 December 2020). [2]

# Annex 2.A. Composition of the Advisory Council

The Advisory Council is a collegiate body, composed of the members provided for in article 41 of ERSE's Statutes (representatives of regulated companies, market suppliers, several consumer associations, the Competition Authority and municipalities), appointed in accordance with the rules established in Regulation 628/2019, of 9 August, for a renewable period of three years.

The electricity section is composed of the representatives indicated in a) to s) below, as well as the representatives of the regional governments, electricity sector companies and consumers of the Autonomous Regions.

The natural gas section is composed of the representatives identified in a) to j), p) and t) to z) below.

The Advisory Council is composed as follows:

a) President: personality of recognised merit and independence to be appointed by the Government member responsible for energy
b) One representative of the Government member responsible for finance
c) One representative of the Government member responsible for the environment
d) One representative of the Government member responsible for energy
e) One representative of the National Association of Portuguese Municipalities
f) One representative of the Directorate-General for Energy and Geology
g) One representative of the Directorate-General for Consumer Affairs
h) One representative of the Competition Authority
i) One representative of the Portuguese Environment Agency, IPA
j) Three representatives of consumer protection associations that represent consumers in general, pursuant to Law No. 24/1996 of 31 July, as currently worded.
k) One representative of the entities holding binding electricity generation licenses under the ordinary regime
l) One representative of the associations of Portuguese producers of electricity from renewable energy sources
m) One representative of the concession holder of the National Electricity Transmission Grid
n) One representative of the concession holder of the National Electricity Distribution Grid
o) One representative of the concession holders of electricity distribution at low voltage (LV)
p) One representative of the logistic operator of switching supplier of electricity and natural gas
q) One representative of the supplier of last resort for electricity who operates in that capacity throughout the continent
r) One representative of suppliers of electricity subject to free trade
s) One representative of the associations whose members are consumers of electricity at medium voltage (MV), high voltage (HV) and very high voltage (EHV)
t) One representative of the concession holder of the National Natural Gas Transmission Grid
u) One representative of the concession holders of the activities of reception, storage and re-gasification of liquefied natural gas (LNG)

v) One representative of the entities holding concessions for the regional natural gas distribution networks
w) One representative of the holders of public service natural gas distribution licences
x) One representative of supplier of last resort for natural gas
y) One representative of suppliers of natural gas subject to free trade
z) One representative of the associations whose members are natural gas customers with annual consumption exceeding 10 000 m3.

The following are also members of the Advisory Council:

a) One representative of the Regional Government of the Azores
b) One representative of the Regional Government of Madeira
c) One representative of consumers of the Autonomous Region of the Azores
d) One representative of consumers of the Autonomous Region of Madeira
e) One representative of the electricity system companies of the Autonomous Region of the Azores
f) One representative of the electricity system companies of the Autonomous Region of Madeira.

# Annex 2.B. Composition of the Tariff Council

The Tariff Council is a collegiate body, composed of the members provided for in article 46 of ERSE's Statutes (representatives of regulated companies, market suppliers, several consumer associations, the Competition Authority and municipalities), appointed in accordance with the rules established in Regulation 628/2019, of 9 August, for a renewable period of three years.

The Tariff Council has two sections: one for the electricity sector and one for the natural gas sector.

The electricity section is composed by the representatives indicated in a) to k) and u) to y) below. The natural gas section is composed by the representatives indicated in a) to e) and l) to u) below.

The Tariff Council is composed as follows:

a) President: personality of recognised merit and independence to be appointed by the Government member responsible for energy.
b) A personality of recognised merit and independence to be appointed by the Government member responsible for environmental department.
c) One representative of the National Association of Portuguese Municipalities.
d) Three representatives of consumer protection associations that represent consumers in general, pursuant to Law No. 24/96 of 31 July, as currently worded.
e) One representative of the Directorate-General for Consumer Affairs.
f) One representative of the associations whose members are consumers of electricity at medium voltage (MV), high voltage (HV) and very high voltage (EHV).
g) One representative of the concession holder of the National Electricity Transmission Grid.
h) One representative of the concession holder of the National Electricity Distribution Grid.
i) One representative of the concession holders of electricity distribution in low voltage (LV).
j) One representative of supplier of last resort for electricity who operates in that capacity throughout the continent.
k) One representative of suppliers of electricity subject to free trade.
l) One representative of the concession holder of the National Natural Gas Transmission Grid.
m) One representative of the concession holders of the activities of reception, storage and re-gasification of liquefied natural gas (LNG).
n) One representative of the concession holders of the underground storage of natural gas.
o) One representative of the entities holding concessions for the regional natural gas distribution networks.
p) One representative of the holders of public service natural gas distribution licenses.
q) One representative of the supplier of last resort for natural gas (retail).
r) One representative of the supplier of last resort supplier of natural gas (wholesale).
s) One representative of suppliers of natural gas subject to free trade.
t) One representative of the associations whose members are natural gas customers with annual consumption exceeding 10 000 $m^3$.
u) One representative of small energy traders.
v) One representative of consumers of the Autonomous Region of the Azores.

w) One representative of consumers of the Autonomous Region of Madeira.

x) One representative of the electricity system companies of the Autonomous Region of the Azores.

y) One representative of the electricity system companies of the Autonomous Region of Madeira.

# Annex 2.C. Composition of the Fuels Council

The Fuels Council is a collegiate body, composed of the members provided for in article 44-B of ERSE's Statutes, appointed in accordance with the rules established in Regulation 628/2019 of 9 August, for a renewable three-year term of office.

The Fuels Council has two sections: one for petroleum-derived fuel sector and one for biofuels sector. The petroleum-derived fuel section is composed by the representatives indicated in a) to k) below. The biofuels section is composed by the representatives indicated in a) and l) to t) below.

a) President: Person of recognised standing and independence appointed by the member of the Government responsible for energy
b) Representative of *Associação Portuguesa de Empresas Petrolíferas* (APETRO – the Portuguese Association of Oil Companies) – section of the petroleum-derived fuel and biofuel sectors
c) Representative of *Associação Portuguesa de Produtores de Biocombustíveis* (APPB – the Portuguese Association of Biofuel Producers)
d) Representative of *Associação Nacional dos Revendedores de Combustíveis* (ANAREC – the Portuguese Association of Fuel Retailers) – section of the petroleum-derived fuel and biofuel sectors
e) Representative of *Associação de Empresas Distribuidoras de Produtos Petrolíferos* (EDIP – the Portuguese Association of Petroleum Product Distributors) – section of the petroleum-derived fuel and biofuel sectors
f) Representative of *Associação Portuguesa das Empresas de Distribuição* (APED – the Portuguese Association of Distribution Companies) – section of the petroleum-derived fuel and biofuel sectors
g) Representative of general interest consumer associations (DECO) – section of the petroleum-derived fuel and biofuel sectors
h) Representative of *Automóvel Clube de Portugal* (ACP – the Portuguese Automobile Club) – section of the petroleum-derived fuel and biofuel sectors
i) Representative of national associations of the sector of road transport powered by petroleum products – section of the petroleum-derived fuel and biofuel sectors
j) Representative of *Confederação da Indústria Portuguesa* (CIP – the Portuguese Industry Confederation) – section of the petroleum-derived fuel and biofuel sectors
k) Representative of *Confederação dos Agricultores Portugueses* (CAP – the Portuguese Farmers Confederation) – section of the petroleum-derived fuel and biofuel sectors
l) Representative of *Associação Portuguesa de Empresas Petrolíferas* (APETRO) – section of the liquefied petroleum gas sector
m) Representative of *Associação Nacional dos Revendedores de Combustíveis* (ANAREC) – section of the liquefied petroleum gas sector
n) Representative of *Associação de Empresas Distribuidoras de Produtos Petrolíferos* (EDIP) – section of the liquefied petroleum gas sector
o) Representative of *Associação Portuguesa das Empresas de Distribuição* (APED) – section of the liquefied petroleum gas sector
p) Representative of piped propane gas distribution operators – section of the liquefied petroleum gas sector

q) Representative of general interest consumer associations (UGC) – section of the liquefied petroleum gas sector

r) Two representatives of associations representing LPG-consuming economic activities – section of the liquefied petroleum gas sector

s) Representative of *Automóvel Clube de Portugal* (ACP) [the Portuguese Automobile Club] – section of the liquefied petroleum gas sector

t) Representative of *Confederação da Indústria Portuguesa* (CIP) – section of the liquefied petroleum gas sector.

# Annex A. Methodology

Measuring regulatory performance is challenging, starting with defining what to measure, dealing with confounding factors, attributing outcomes to interventions and coping with the lack of data and information. This chapter describes the methodology developed by the OECD to help regulators address these challenges through a Performance Assessment Framework for Economic Regulators (PAFER), which informs this review. The chapter first presents some of the work conducted by the OECD on measuring regulatory performance. It then describes the key features of the PAFER and presents a typology of performance indicators to measure input, process, output and outcome. It finally provides an overview of the approach and practical steps undertaken for developing this review.

This Annex summarises the methodology developed by the OECD to assess regulatory authorities' governance arrangements, drivers of performance as well as their performance measurement matrices. The methodology was prepared based on the experience of regulators participating in the OECD Network of Economic Regulators and the present report constitutes its twelfth application to a regulatory body. Other reviews spanning a number of sectors and countries include: Colombia's Communications Regulation Commission (OECD, 2015[1]), Latvia's Public Utilities Commission (OECD, 2016[2]), Mexico's three energy regulators (OECD, 2017[3]); (OECD, 2017[4]); (OECD, 2017[5]); (OECD, 2017[6]), Ireland's Commission for Regulation of Utilities (OECD, 2018[7]); Peru's Energy and Mining Regulator (OECD, 2019[8]); Peru's Telecommunications Regulator (OECD, 2019[9]), Peru's Transport Infrastructure Regulator (OECD, 2020[10])and Ireland's Environmental Protection Agency (OECD, 2020[11]). The methodology has been adapted since its first application to learnings throughout the review process and is adjusted to take into account specific needs and contextual characteristics of each regulator, sector and jurisdiction.

## Analytical framework

The analytical framework that informs this review draws on the work conducted by the OECD on measuring regulatory performance and the governance of economic regulators. OECD countries and regulators have recognised the need for measuring regulatory performance. Information on regulatory performance is necessary to better target scarce resources and to improve the overall performance of regulatory policies and regulators. However, measuring regulatory performance can prove challenging. Some of these challenges include:

- *What to measure*: evaluation systems require an assessment of how inputs have influenced outputs and outcomes. In the case of regulatory policy, the inputs can focus on: i) overall programmes intended to promote a systemic improvement of regulatory quality; ii) the application of specific practices intended to improve regulation, or, iii) changes in the design of specific regulations.
- *Confounding factors*: there is a myriad of contingent issues that have an impact on the outcomes in society which regulation is intended to affect. These issues can be as simple as a change in the weather, or as complicated as the last financial crisis. Accordingly, it is difficult to establish a direct causal relationship between the adoption of better regulation practices and specific improvements to the welfare outcomes that are sought in the economy.
- *Lack of data and information*: countries tend to lack data and methodologies to identify whether regulatory practices are being undertaken correctly and what impact these practices may be having on the real economy.

The OECD (2014[12]) *Framework for Regulatory Policy Evaluation* starts addressing these challenges through an input-process-output-outcome logic, which breaks down the regulatory process into a sequence of discrete steps. The input-process-output-outcome logic is flexible and can be applied both to evaluate practices to improve regulatory policy in general, and also to evaluate regulatory policy in specific sectors, based on the identification of relevant strategic objectives. It can be tailored to economic regulators by taking into consideration the conditions that support the performance of economic regulators (Box A A.1).

The OECD Best Practice Principles for Regulatory Policy: The Governance of Regulators (OECD, 2014[13]) identifies some of the conditions that support the performance of economic regulators. They recognise the importance of assessing how a regulator is directed, controlled, resourced and held to account, in order to improve the overall effectiveness of regulators and promote growth and investment, including by supporting competition. Moreover, they acknowledge the positive impact of the regulator's own internal process on outcomes (i.e. how the regulator manages resources and what processes the regulator puts in place to regulate a given sector or market) (Figure A A.1).

**Box A A.1. The input-process-output-outcome logic sequence**

- Step I. Input: indicators include for example the budget and staff of the regulatory oversight body.
- Step II. Process: indicators assess whether formal requirements for good regulatory practices are in place. This includes requirements for objective setting, consultation, evidence-based analysis, administrative simplification, risk assessments and aligning regulatory changes internationally.
- Step III. Output: indicators provide information on whether the good regulatory practices have actually been implemented.
- Step IV. Impact of design on outcome (also referred to as intermediate outcome): indicators assess whether good regulatory practices contributed to an improvement in the quality of regulations. It therefore attempts to make a causal link between the design of regulatory policy and outcomes.
- Step V. Strategic outcomes: indicators assess whether the desired outcomes of regulatory policy have been achieved, both in terms of regulatory quality and in terms of regulatory outcomes.

Source: (OECD, 2014[12]).

**Figure A A.1. The OECD Best Practice Principles on the Governance of Regulators**

Source: Adapted from (OECD, 2014[13]).

The two frameworks are brought together into a Performance Assessment Framework for Economic Regulators that structures the drivers of performance along the input-process-output-outcome framework (Table A A.1).

**Table A A.1. Criteria for assessing regulators' own performance framework**

| References | Strategic objectives | Input | Process | Output and outcome |
|---|---|---|---|---|
| Best Practice Principles for the Governance of Regulators | • Role clarity | • Funding | • Maintaining trust and preventing undue influence | • Performance evaluation |
| | | | • Decision making and governing body structure | |
| | | | • Accountability and transparency | |
| | | | • Engagement | |
| Institutional, organisational and monitoring drivers | • Objectives and targets | • Budgeting and financial management | • Strategy, leadership and co-ordination | • Performance standards and indicators |
| | • Functions and powers | • Human resources management | • Institutional structure | • Performance processes and reports |
| | | | • Management systems and operating processes | • Feedback or outside evidence on performance |
| | | | • Relations and interfaces with Government bodies, regulated entities and other key stakeholders | |
| | | | • Regulatory management tools | |

Source: OECD Analysis.

## Performance indicators

For regulators, performance indicators need to fit the purpose of performance assessment, which is a systematic, analytical evaluation of the regulator's activities, with the purpose of seeking reliability and usability of the regulator's activities. Performance assessment is neither an audit, which judges how employees and managers complete their mission, nor a control, which puts emphasis on compliance with standards (OECD, 2004[14]).

Accordingly, performance indicators need to assess the efficient and effective use of a regulator's inputs, the quality of regulatory processes, and identify outputs and some direct outcomes that can be attributed to the regulator's interventions. Wider outcomes should serve as a "watchtower", which provides the information the regulator can use to identify problem areas, orient decisions and identify priorities (Figure A A.2).

Figure A A.2. Input-process-output-outcome framework for performance indicators

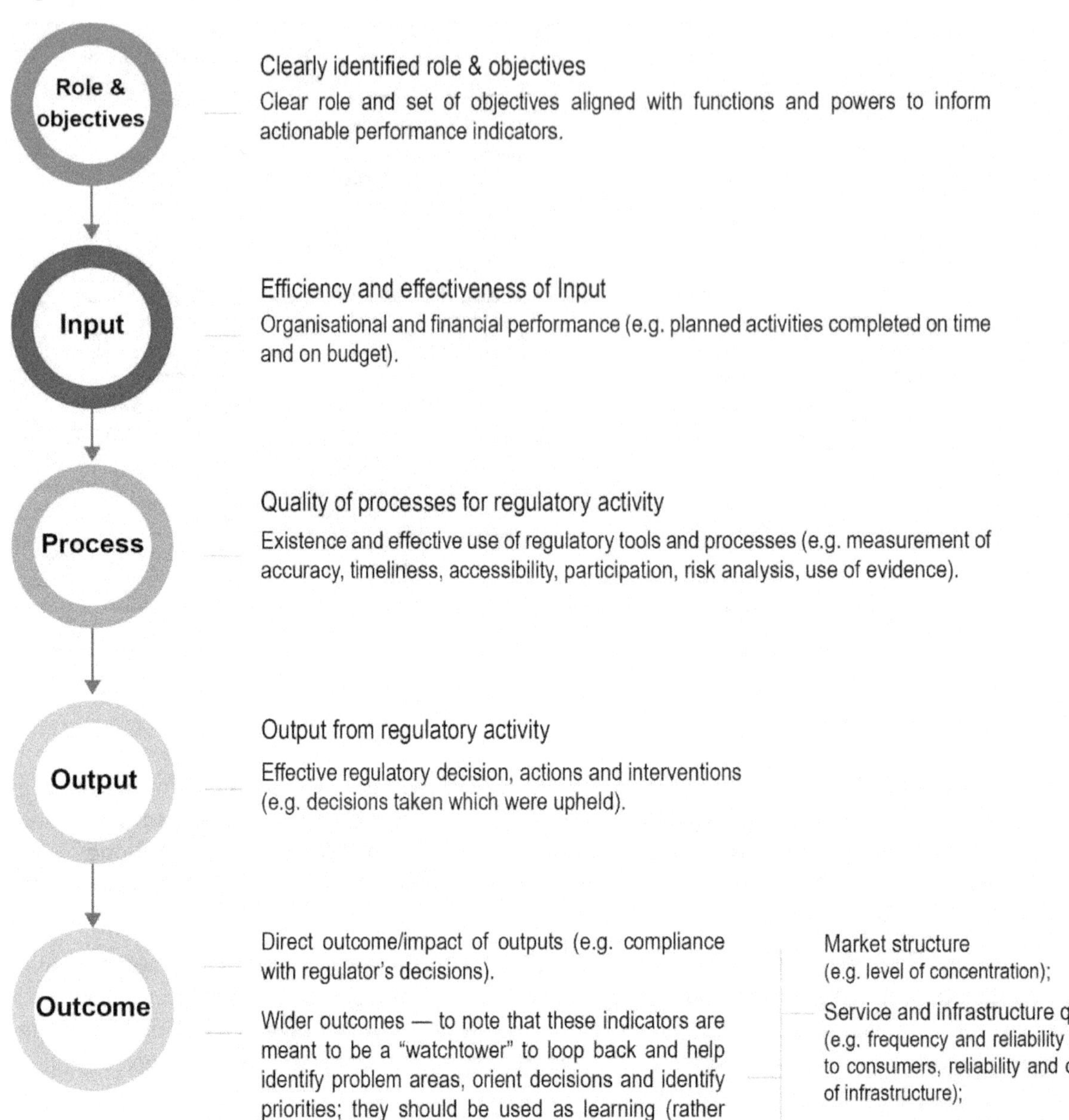


Notes: This framework was proposed in the initial methodology for the performance assessment framework for economic regulators (PAFER) discussed with the OECD Network of Economic Regulators (NER). It has been refined to reflect feedback from NER members and the experience of other regulators in assessing their own performance.
Source: (OECD, 2015[1]), Figure 3.3 (updated in 2017).

## Approach

The analytical framework presented above informed the data collection and the analysis presented in the report. The present report looks at the internal and external governance arrangements of Portugal's Energy Services Regulatory Authority (ERSE) in the following areas:

- ***Role and objectives***: to identify the existence of a set of clearly identified objectives, targets, or goals that are aligned with the regulator's functions and powers, which can inform the development of actionable performance indicators;
- ***Input***: to determine the extent to which the regulator's funding and staffing are aligned with the regulator's objectives, targets or goals, and the regulator's ability to manage financial and human resources autonomously and effectively;
- ***Process***: to assess the extent to which processes and the organisational management support the regulator's performance;
- ***Output and outcome***: to identify the existence of a systematic assessment of the performance of the regulated entities, the impact of the regulator's decisions and activities, and the extent to which these measurements are used appropriately.

Data informing the analysis presented in the report was collected via a desk review, two fact-finding missions and a peer mission:

- ***Questionnaire and desk review***: ERSE completed a detailed questionnaire which informed a desk review by the OECD Secretariat. The Secretariat reviewed existing legislation and ERSE documents to collect information on the *de jure* functioning of the regulator, and to inform the fact-finding missions. This questionnaire was tailored to ERSE, based on the methodology already applied by the OECD to other regulators since 2015 and on the participation of ERSE to former OECD data collection exercises such as the 2018 Indicators on the Governance of Sector Regulators.
- ***Fact-finding missions***: the first fact-finding mission focused on meeting ERSE internal teams and was conducted by the OECD Secretariat between 8-10 January 2020. The second fact-finding mission took place between 11-14 February 2020 and focused primarily on meeting external stakeholders. These missions were the key tool to collect and complete the *de jure* information obtained through the questionnaire with the *de facto* state of play. The work of the fact-finding missions tailored the PAFER methodology to ERSE features. Information collected was completed and checked with ERSE for accuracy. Both missions took place in Lisbon.
- ***Peer mission***: the mission took place between 15-18 June 2020 and included peer reviewers from Australia, Ireland and Sweden, in addition to the OECD Secretariat. This mission met with key stakeholders in ERSE as well as externally. At the end of the mission, the team discussed preliminary findings and recommendations with senior management from ERSE to test their feasibility. This mission was conducted remotely via videoconference due to the context of the COVID-19 pandemic .

During the fact-finding and peer missions, the team met with ERSE's leadership team as well as a number of staff from across the institution. In addition, the team met with government institutions and external stakeholders, including:

- Ministry for Environment and Climate Action (MAAC)
- Directorate-General for Energy and Geology (DGEG)
- Directorate-General for Consumer Affairs
- Competition Authority (AdC)
- Portuguese Securities Market Commission (CMVM)

- National Authority for Communications (ANACOM)
- A Member of the Portuguese Parliament
- National Entity for Energy Sector (ENSE)
- Presidents of ERSE's Advisory Council, Tariff Council and Fuels Council
- Azores and Madeira regional governments and company representatives
- REN Group: TSO gas (REN Gasodutos), TSO electricity (REN Eléctrica), and DSO gas (REN Portgás)
- EDP Group: Producer and DSO for electricity
- Wholesale platform for the Iberian Energy Market (OMIP)
- Consumer protection organisation, DECO and DECO Proteste
- Confederation of Portuguese Business (CIP)
- Portuguese Renewable Energy Association (APREN)
- Association of energy traders in the liberalised market (ACEMEL)
- Jorge Vasconcelosa, former ERSE president
- Manuel Cabugueira, Co-ordinator of the Technical Unit for Legislative Impact Assessment and member of the Portugal Delegation to the Regulatory Policy Committee

## References

OECD (2020), *Driving Performance at Ireland's Environmental Protection Agency*, The Governance of Regulators, OECD Publishing, Paris, https://dx.doi.org/10.1787/009a0785-en. [11]

OECD (2020), *Driving Performance at Peru's Transport Infrastructure Regulator*, The Governance of Regulators, OECD Publishing, Paris, https://dx.doi.org/10.1787/d4ddab52-en. [10]

OECD (2019), *Driving Performance at Peru's Energy and Mining Regulator*, The Governance of Regulators, OECD Publishing, Paris, https://dx.doi.org/10.1787/9789264310865-en. [8]

OECD (2019), *Driving Performance at Peru's Telecommunications Regulator*, The Governance of Regulators, OECD Publishing, Paris, https://dx.doi.org/10.1787/9789264310506-en. [9]

OECD (2018), *Driving Performance at Ireland's Commission for Regulation of Utilities*, The Governance of Regulators, OECD Publishing, Paris, http://dx.doi.org/10.1787/9789264190061-en. [7]

OECD (2017), *Driving Performance at Mexico's Agency for Safety, Energy and Environment*, The Governance of Regulators, OECD Publishing, Paris, https://dx.doi.org/10.1787/9789264280458-en. [6]

OECD (2017), *Driving Performance at Mexico's Energy Regulatory Commission*, The Governance of Regulators, OECD Publishing, Paris, https://dx.doi.org/10.1787/9789264280830-en. [4]

OECD (2017), *Driving Performance at Mexico's National Hydrocarbons Commission*, The Governance of Regulators, OECD Publishing, Paris, https://dx.doi.org/10.1787/9789264280748-en. [5]

OECD (2017), *Driving Performance of Mexico's Energy Regulators*, The Governance of Regulators, OECD Publishing, Paris, https://dx.doi.org/10.1787/9789264267848-en. [3]

OECD (2016), *Driving Performance at Latvia's Public Utilities Commission*, The Governance of Regulators, OECD Publishing, Paris, https://dx.doi.org/10.1787/9789264257962-en. [2]

OECD (2015), *Driving Performance at Colombia's Communications Regulator*, OECD Publishing, Paris, https://dx.doi.org/10.1787/9789264232945-en. [1]

OECD (2014), *OECD Framework for Regulatory Policy Evaluation*, OECD Publishing, Paris, https://dx.doi.org/10.1787/9789264214453-en. [12]

OECD (2014), *The Governance of Regulators*, OECD Best Practice Principles for Regulatory Policy, OECD Publishing, Paris, https://dx.doi.org/10.1787/9789264209015-en. [13]

OECD (2004), *The choice of tools for enhancing policy impact: Evaluation and review*, OECD, Paris, http://www.oecd.org/officialdocuments/publicdisplaydocumentpdf/?cote=gov/pgc(2004)4&doclanguage=en (accessed on 16 November 2018). [14]

www.ingramcontent.com/pod-product-compliance
Lightning Source LLC
LaVergne TN
LVHW061249100826
845148LV00008B/1073
*9789264911529*